MW01009368

Bogie and Betty: The Lives and Legacies of Humphrey Bogart and Lauren Bacall

By Charles River Editors

Humphrey Bogart and Lauren Bacall in *Dark Passage* (1947)

About Charles River Editors

Charles River Editors provides superior editing and original writing services across the digital publishing industry, with the expertise to create digital content for publishers across a vast range of subject matter. In addition to providing original digital content for third party publishers, we also republish civilization's greatest literary works, bringing them to new generations of readers via ebooks.

Introduction

Humphrey Bogart (1899-1957)

"All you owe the public is a good performance." – Humphrey Bogart

Americans have always loved movie stars, and there have been no shortage of Hollywood icons, but one man has long been considered the greatest male star. From the time he first became a leading man, Humphrey Bogart's screen image has resonated with viewers more than perhaps any other actor. At the end of the 20th century, when the American Film Institute assembled its list of the 50 Greatest American Screen Legends, Bogart was at the top of the list. His persona as a tough guy who manages to maintain his sense of virtue no matter how compromising the situation features in some of the most famous films ever made, including *Casablanca* (1942), *The Maltese Falcon* (1941), and *Key Largo* (1949).

Bogart's screen persona was not only desirable (everyone wanted to be like Bogart) but also highly approachable, in the sense that he played the everyman figure far more than Cary Grant or Laurence Olivier, for example. Bogart also had good timing, with some of his popularity due to the fact that he rose to fame in an era when the film industry was at its most potent. Bogart's prime coincided with the Golden Age of cinema; sound had been successfully integrated and the studio system ruled over the industry. Bogart was the biggest star at a time in which the medium itself held immense mass appeal, and he has been famous ever since.

People have long been familiar with Bogart's career and movies, but the differences between his persona and his real life are also interesting. Bogart's everyman screen persona belies the fact that he came from immense privilege, and his down-to-earth film roles are in many ways a rebellion against a family with which he was never close. There were traits that Bogart inherited from his parents, but his film career also offered Bogart to escape a family culture that was antithetical to his personality. Bogart's screen persona as a jaded but ultimately indestructible figure also obscures the fact that his life was filled with substantial tragedy, culminating in his own premature death at the age of 57. Separating Bogart's real life from his reel life is still a subject of great interest and debate.

Bogie and Betty profiles the life, career, and legacy of the man deemed by the American Film Institute as the greatest male star. Along with pictures of important people, places, and events, you will learn about Humphrey Bogart like you never have before.

Bacall's studio shot from the 1940s.

Lauren Bacall (1924-)

"Imagination is the highest kite that can fly." – Lauren Bacall

A lot of ink has been spilled covering the lives of history's most influential figures, but how much of the forest is lost for the trees? In Charles River Editors' American Legends series, readers can get caught up to speed on the lives of America's most important men and women in the time it takes to finish a commute, while learning interesting facts long forgotten or never known.

It is exceedingly difficult to think about Lauren Bacall without also thinking of her famous husband, Humphrey Bogart. After all, it is no accident that Bacall was entirely unknown before starring at just 20 years old with her future husband in Howard Hawks' famous film *To Have and Have Not* in 1944. And of course, Bogart's infatuation with the young actress helped ensure she would continue to be cast in movies with him moving forward. "Bogie and Bacall" are just one of a number of legendary romantic screen duos in film history, and there have been other famous screen couples who made headlines off the set as well, but few compare in terms of success. In the wake of their first film together, Bacall and Bogart captivated audiences in other films during the decade, including *The Big Sleep (1946), Dark Victory (1947),* and finally, *Key Largo* (1948). Even though they did not appear in a large number of films together, the popularity and cultural significance of these films solidified the status of "Bogie and Bacall" as one of the premier romantic couples in film history.

When Bogart died in 1957, Bacall was still in her 30s, yet from 1957 onward her name scarcely surfaces in popular culture, as though Bacall was simply wiped away with her late husband. In fact, it often comes as a great surprise to people that Bacall is still alive and well as she nears her 90th birthday. For her part, Bacall has remained at least partially in the public eye through her own meticulous documentation of her life, captured through two detailed memoirs (the first published in the late 1970s, the second published in 2005.) It is true that Bacall never reached anything close to the heights of the fame she enjoyed with Bogart, but she appeared in many movies in the years after his death and was even involved in a second high-profile marriage with actor Jason Robards from 1961-1969. She has remained active well into old age and never officially retired; in fact, she held a starring role in the 2012 film *The Forger*.

Bogie and Betty examines each period of Bacall's life, addressing her life before, during, and after her relationship with Humphrey Bogart. In particular, her life and career illuminate many pertinent areas of cinema and American culture, and the role of women in film and society. Along with pictures of important people, places, and events, you will learn about Lauren Bacall like never before.

Chapter 1: Bogart's Early Years

One of the most shocking aspects of Humphrey Bogart's life story is the discrepancy between his roles on screen and his family background. Humphrey was the eldest child of Belmont DeForest Bogart and Maud Humphrey, and he would later have two younger sisters, Frances and Catherine. Humphrey's father was a Presbyterian with Dutch and English ancestry whose last name was Dutch for "keeper of an orchard", but Belmont worked as a cardiopulmonary surgeon and came from a privileged family background. He had also descended from a family with historical ties to the landscape, as his family had arrived in Brooklyn from Holland in the 17th century. Humphrey's grandfather, Adam Watkins Bogart, ran an inn in the Finger Lakes region in upstate New York, and in 1853 the family had relocated to upstate New York from Brooklyn. Adam descended from a lineage of farmers, but Humphrey's paternal grandmother had come from a wealthy background herself.

Belmont was born in 1866, just one year following the death of his brother. His mother would die just two years after his birth and left all of her wealth to her son. But interestingly, in her will she asked that Belmont be removed from her husband's possession and placed in the custody of one of her sisters. Adam eventually sued her estate and won, regaining custody over his son. With his inheritance, Belmont was sure to enjoy a comfortable upbringing, and his father Adam made a fortune from creating a method for lithographing plates, but the unusual episode surrounding the will and Belmont's custody demonstrated the coldness of his parents' marriage. That lack of affection would also be especially relevant in Humphrey Bogart's life.

It is believed that Humphrey was born on Christmas Day in 1899, but the story has faced much dissension over the years because it seemed too good to be true. For a long time, many people thought Humphrey's Christmas Day birthday was a myth fabricated by Warner Brothers to add to his allure. The alternative theory was that he was born in late January 1900, but documents from the period suggest he was definitely born in December 1899. While movie studios often changed their stars' names and other pertinent information, based on his movie roles it would seem as though Bogart lacked the kind of sweet nature that would drive the studio to fabricate that story out of thin air.

Bogart's unusual first name was borrowed from his mother's maiden name. Maud Humphrey was of English origin and Episcopalian faith. She was also considered an extraordinarily beautiful woman, with vivid red hair. Her father was a wealthy shoe manufacturer, and she grew up even more privileged than her husband. Given the era Maud grew up in, she was a very strong and career-oriented woman, and she was also an avowed suffragette who never submitted to the male-dominated norms of the time period.

Maud's parents had sent her to art school, where she became an accomplished illustrator. After graduating from school and marrying Belmont, she worked as a commercial illustrator, where she earned a robust salary of $50,000 per year, more than double her husband's not-insignificant salary. Naturally, Maud drew pictures of her baby boy, one of which was featured in an ad campaign for Mellins Baby Food. Humphrey would later wryly note, "There was a period in American history when you couldn't pick up a goddamned magazine without seeing my kisser in it."

Maud and Humphrey

Humphrey as a boy

Since they were each so independently driven, Bogart's parents were never close or affectionate, and they sparred continuously, unleashing sarcastic quips on each other that made them seem more like rivals than loving parents. Humphrey clearly inherited his own caustic wit from his parents, but as a young child he suffered from lack of attention. As Humphrey put it, "I was brought up very unsentimentally but very straightforwardly. A kiss, in our family, was an event. Our mother and father didn't glug over my two sisters and me."

In fact, with his parents constantly working, Humphrey was largely raised by a collection of housekeepers and caretakers. His parents eschewed all manner of physical or verbal affection, keeping a cold distance from him that would never grow more intimate, even after their son rose to fame. Humphrey explained, "If, when I was grown up, I sent my mother one of those Mother's Day telegrams or said it with flowers, she would have returned the wire and flowers to me, collect."

Despite their professional strength and standing in the New York society realm, Humphrey's parents were physically fragile figures. Maud suffered from debilitating headaches, while Belmont was addicted to morphine, a condition that would later play a strong role in his demise. When both were at home, they continuously fought with one another, no doubt in part due to the fact that they often didn't feel well.

Of course, Humphrey's privileged upbringing had enormous advantages that were counterbalanced by significant disadvantages. He came from a highly respected family that lived in a posh Upper West Side apartment in Manhattan and was listed in *Dua's New York Blue Book*. The block Humphrey grew up on has since been ceremonially renamed Humphrey Bogart Place. Naturally there were aspects of his family's wealth that Humphrey enjoyed. Chief among these was the family's summer stays at their 55-acre estate in Canandaigua in upstate New York. The family held a prominent role in the summer community, and their arrival and departure was fodder for the newspaper. While summering, he was introduced to major society figures, including future president Franklin Delano Roosevelt.

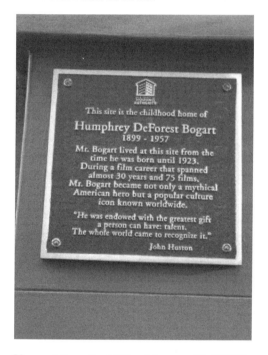

Plaque at Bogart's childhood home on W. 103rd St.

In 1913, when Bogart was still 13 years old, his family switched summer homes, relocating to Fire Island in order to be closer to Maud's job in New York City. In 1910, she had assumed the prestigious role of artistic director for the fashion magazine *The Delineator*. At Fire Island, Bogart became friends with the other residents, staged theatrical productions with them, and met his first girlfriend there. One of his closest friends was William Brady Jr., who would play an instrumental role later in his life. Brady was the closest friend Bogart would have during his youth, and the two were given free tickets to Broadway shows by Brady's father, entertainment mogul William Brady Sr. It has even been suggested that the friendship between Bogart and Brady was at times homoerotic. Most importantly, summering on the water engendered a deep love for boating, and Humphrey became particularly adept at sailing, a passion that would remain with him for the rest of his life.

Humphrey was quite happy during the summer, but he lived in relative misery during the other parts of the year. The thing that stood out most about young Humphrey was that his mother insisted on dressing him in precious clothes that had long become antiquated by the time he was born. Humphrey also grew to resent his name, which quickly became a source of ridicule among his classmates. Making matters worse, another source of self-consciousness stemmed from the fact that as a young child, Maud had illustrated her son in the nude from behind, a drawing that became famous and was disseminated throughout the country. Although Maud refrained from giving her son loving attention and their relationship was quite distant, it is also apparent that Humphrey was monitored too closely by his mother, who did not give him the agency to dress and present himself in a manner that would endear him to his classmates. His famous lisp, which would later become one of his trademarks as an actor, caused ridicule from his classmates, as did his curly hair. As a result, Humphrey was perpetually viewed as a pretty boy and an outsider; one classmate said of him, "Bogart never came out for anything. He wasn't a very good student... He added up to nothing in our class."

Given that his time at school was another source of discomfort, it is no surprise that Humphrey shunned his studies even at an early age. At first, he attended the Delancey School, where he matriculated until the 5th grade. Bogart then enrolled in Trinity School, an elite all-boys school that had already been in existence for 200 years by the time Humphrey went there in 1909. While attending Trinity School, Bogart was required to don a blue suit, a style of dress he would retain for the rest of his life. He attended Trinity for a full 8 years, during which time he performed poorly and was forced to repeat the 11th grade after having suffered from scarlet fever. After returning from school, Humphrey would pose for his mother, who would draw him in her studio. This curious dynamic, in which Humphrey was fodder for her illustrations, has led plenty of people to suggest that Humphrey's first experience as an actor was in his own home.

Despite attending prestigious schools, Humphrey always believed that school was not the appropriate environment for him. Even so, his parents had high aspirations that he would follow in his father's footsteps and become a doctor, so there was immense pressure on Bogart to perform well in school. The family also regularly entertained literary luminaries like Theodore Dreiser and H.L. Mencken, and Humphrey was an articulate and avid reader, so his lack of academic success greatly frustrated his parents. In a sense, his perpetual lack of achievement in school was a form of rebellion against his parents and his early years more than an expression of poor intelligence.

By the time Bogart neared the end of his high school studies, it was clear that he would need assistance in order to gain admittance to a prestigious college. Therefore, Belmont used his connections to have Humphrey admitted at Philips Andover Academy in Massachusetts, where Humphrey was to matriculate for his final year of high school and eventually attend medical school at Yale University. However, Belmont's best-laid plans were not realized, and the year at Andover was a tumultuous whirlwind of interactions between Humphrey, Belmont, and the school's headmaster. Ultimately, Humphrey was expelled just one month before graduating and was offered no option to repeat the year.

School was clearly a source of unhappiness for Humphrey, so his expulsion from Andover would come to be a welcome occurrence for him, especially because it effectively terminated his parents' delusional view that their son would grow up to be a surgeon. After failing to complete even the one year at Andover, they were finally forced to acknowledge that school was not the proper venue for their son. In this regard, the year at Andover was a sort of success for Humphrey.

Chapter 2: Bogart on His Own

"At 18, war was great stuff. Paris! French girls! Hot damn!...The war was a big joke. Death? What does death mean to a 17 year old?" – Humphrey Bogart

After his year ended prematurely at Andover, Maud secured her son a job working for a naval architect. Uninterested in this line of work, or in having his parents decide his profession, Humphrey lasted a very short time there; in fact, some people assert that he never actually worked there at all. In an act of youthful exuberance and rebellion against his parents, Bogart instead decided to enlist in the Navy.

Bogart in the Navy

For someone who had vehemently resisted authority all throughout his life, it may initially come as a surprise that he would choose to enlist in the Navy, which meant he would have to obey authority. However, Bogart knew that he loved ships, and he also wanted to travel overseas and explore the world. In the early summer of 1918, he enlisted and was stationed at the Naval Reserve Training Station in Pelham Bay, off the coast of New York.

While at Pelham Bay, Bogart was unable to progress through the ranks and eventually applied for a transfer to the Naval Aviation branch, but he was denied admission. In reality, Bogart's glamorous fantasies about World War I were ill-founded. By the time he enlisted, the Armistice had already been signed, and he eventually joined the USS *Leviathan*, where he spent 8 months transporting troops back and forth from overseas. It was the least glamorous naval job imaginable, but Bogart finally acquired a sense of discipline and commitment, and there is every indication that his experience there was vastly preferable to his time at Andover and Trinity.

Humphrey may also have received the scarred lip that became his trademark while serving on the *Leviathan*. The most common tale claims that a prisoner of war hit Bogart in the face with his handcuffs while being transferred to Kittery, Maine, but that story has not been verified and there are many conflicting reports, including one that asserts his lip was hit by a piece of shrapnel. Actor David Niven claimed Bogart told him his lip was scarred as a child and the Navy story was made up by movie studios to add to Bogart's persona. Either way, the scarred lip also contributed to Bogart's lisp.

In 1919, Bogart was transferred to the USS *Santa Oliva*, but he failed to show up for the boat's departure for Europe, a serious naval offense that earned him the label of Deserter. Bogart admitted to the transgression, but turning himself in to the authorities was not enough to overturn his punishment. He was forced to draw on more desperate measures. Relying on his family's connections with Franklin D. Roosevelt, who was then Assistant Secretary of the Navy, Humphrey contacted the future president. Taking pity on his family acquaintance, Roosevelt exercised his authority and had Bogart's punishment changed to Absent without Leave. For his actions, he was stationed in solitary confinement for three days, the standard punishment for going AWOL, but the lighter punishment allowed Bogart to be honorably discharged. Bogart was even given a medal for his efforts in the service.

After returning from the Navy, Bogart was still just 19 years old, and he still did not possess even a high school education. Making matters worse, his family's economic situation was in shambles. His father's addiction to morphine had become more severe, and he had begun to lose his mental acuity. In a bizarre move, his father had invested in a foolish business opportunity involving timber, losing the family fortune and falling massively into debt. As a last resort, Belmont was relegated to serving as a ship doctor. Nevertheless, Belmont's travails and the collapse of the family's wealth didn't particularly devastate Humphrey; outside of the family's summer home, he had always resented their upper class trimmings. Bogart had never cared for the pretentious ways the family's wealth had provided for the family, even though he had used money and connections to pull strings a few times himself.

Even if his father was unable to subsidize him, Belmont did use his influence to secure his son a job as a bond salesman. After this occupation proved unsuccessful, Humphrey called upon William Brady Sr., the father of his childhood friend. By this point, Brady had become immensely powerful and was looking to spread his empire from the theater to the motion picture industry. He had founded the motion picture company World Films, where he made a fortune capitalizing on the popularity of the seventh art. Brady offered Bogart a position in his office, where he was paid $35 per week, $5 more than he had made as a bond salesman.

Bogart committed himself to the job with greater diligence than any prior period in his life, and he was immediately successful. After just one month in the office, Humphrey was promoted to the role of production manager, a shift that earned him a salary increase to $50 per week. While with World Films, Bogart conducted a number of tasks, including arranging for props and paying the actors. Eventually, he even served as producer and director, and did screenwriting as well.

Although he enjoyed his time at World Films, Bogart was always more interested in acting. As the 1920s progressed, Bogart began appearing in theatrical productions in New York City. It was clear to everyone, including his reluctant parents, that Bogart was a natural actor; in one of his first performances, Belmont noted of his son, "The boy's good, isn't he?" Still, Bogart was unpolished enough at first that it was also apparent he had plenty of work to do yet.

Bogart was drawn to city life, and the acting lifestyle suited him perfectly. He had begun drinking while in high school, but acting allowed him to drink heavily without losing his job. Bogart spent ample time in speakeasies and became increasingly attached to drinking bourbon and smoking cigarettes. He would later quip, "The whole world is three drinks behind. If everyone in the world would take three drinks, we would have no trouble. If Stalin, Truman and everybody else in the world had three drinks right now, we'd all loosen up and we wouldn't need the United Nations."

Bogart had watched his parents drink heavily, but his own heavy drinking was likely due more to his youth and rebellious personality. The fact that Prohibition was just going into effect only encouraged Bogart to drink more. Bogart and William Brady Jr. became notorious for spending most of their nights at speakeasies in New York, and Bogart was able to partially fund his drinking by challenging bar patrons to chess games for $1 each. When he was strapped for money, the young man frequently managed to talk his way into having the owners put his drinks on a long-running tab. Bogart spent so much time at bars that he constantly fell asleep in them, and some contemporaries claimed his scarred lip came from a barroom brawl.

To Bogart's credit, the long nights and heavy drinking didn't stop him from securing relatively consistent acting opportunities. But Humphrey was repeatedly cast in roles that he found disagreeable, performing in what he would later refer to as "White Pants Willie" roles. Ironically, these stage roles represented the antithesis of the rugged characters he would later portray on film, and it seems his family background made it difficult for him to shed the soft, unmasculine roles he kept being assigned on stage.

Bogart may have thought his career was still less than satisfactory, but his personal life underwent significant developments during the 1920s. While acting in a performance of *Drifting* at the Playhouse Theatre in 1922, he met actress Helen Menken, who he would later marry on May 20, 1926 at the Gramercy Park Hotel in New York City.

Helen Menken

Their marriage was doomed from the start and would last roughly 18 months. Menken was 10 years older than him, and her domineering personality clashed with young Bogart's independent streak. The time he spent at bars made adultery much easier, and he admitted, "I had had enough women by the time I was 27 to know what I was looking for in a wife the next time I married."

Despite what he said, the second marriage didn't go much better. Following his divorce, Bogart met Mary Philips, another actress. Philips was closer in age to Bogart and could drink nearly as much as him, something that was actually considered an asset by her husband, but she was similar in many respects to Menken too, particularly her quick temper. Bogart and Philips had known each other since before he had married Menken, after they performed together in a production of *Nerves* at the Comedy Theatre in 1924. He and Mary would remain married for nearly a decade, but their marriage was hardly a happy one. Bogart was perpetually unfaithful and slept with many women, a dynamic that would continue until he met Lauren Bacall nearly two decades later. More noteworthy, the marriage between two strong-willed individuals reproduced the unhappy marital dynamic that had compromised his parents' own marriage. For whatever reason, Bogart's early marriages were filled with the same friction that had subsumed Belmont and Maud, and he was unable to adhere to the strict routines of domestic life.

Mary Philips

Bogart's career was less than ideal during the 1920s, but it was still possible for a stage actor to earn a decent living during most of the decade. However, this would change with the stock market crash and the onset of the Great Depression. Suddenly, the upper-middle class demographic that the industry had relied upon was gone, and stage actors were forced to search for new opportunities. Fortunately, the collapse of the theater coincided with the emergence of the Motion Picture industry, which by this time was in the process of converting to synchronized sound.

There were many reasons for the emergence of film and its ability to flourish even during the Great Depression. First, film had always marketed itself as a more democratic medium than theater; although film borrowed from theater, it also had roots in more traditionally working class forms of entertainment like the circus and the vaudeville stage. From an economic standpoint, movies were cheaper to attend, and even those who were strapped for money were able to save up and see at least one movie a week. Moreover, the inherent dreamlike quality of film, with spectators sitting in a dark movie house, afforded viewers a sense of escape that was not possible in the theater.

At first, Bogart was unsuccessful in finding consistent employment in the movies. He was able to secure minor roles in two Vitaphone shorts, *The Dancing Town* (1928) (which also starred Mary Philips) and *Broadway's Like That* (1930). In the first film, a 20-minute two-reel production, Bogart plays himself. Meanwhile, *Broadway's Like That* involves a girl finding out on the night before her marriage that her husband (played by Bogart) is already married. Despite these two roles, lasting employment evaded him, and Bogart grew increasingly depressed. He was trapped in an unhappy marriage and lacked consistent acting opportunities.

Finally, Bogart was hired by the Fox Film Cooperative in 1930, where he earned a lucrative salary of $750 per week, a substantial amount of money during the Great Depression. He began to appear in films on a continuous basis, but he also acted in the theater as well. He appeared in John Ford's early film *Up the River* (1930), during which he met then-unknown actor Spencer Tracy, who would later become one of his closest friends. The next year, he acted in *The Bad Sister*, playing a minor role in the film, which starred Bette Davis.

Bette Davis

Spencer Tracy

However, after his contract with Fox expired, Bogart again found himself without work and he spiraled into a deep depression. For the next four years, he would alternate between theater and cinema, but he suffered from extended bouts of unemployment the entire time. Bogart continued to drink heavily, and conditions were made even worse when his parents separated and his father died. Belmont's death left Bogart with substantial debt, placing him in a position of outright economic desperation. One friend later recalled seeing Bogart drinking himself into a stupor at a low-scale bar in the city and saying to her friend, "Poor Humphrey, he's finally licked."

Chapter 3: Bacall's Early Years

"A planned life is a dead life." – Lauren Bacall

As Bogart was having trouble breaking into the entertainment industry, the woman he would be most closely associated with was growing up in the same city. Compared with other famous Hollywood stars, Lauren Bacall's childhood was relatively nondescript. She had neither the privileged upbringing of stars like Humphrey Bogart and Katharine Hepburn, nor the hardship experienced by Marilyn Monroe or Judy Garland. But like many of them, her famous screen name was different than the one she was given at birth. She was born Betty Joan Perske on 16 September 1924.

Betty received unconditional love from her mother and support from her extended family as well, yet it would be erroneous to claim that her childhood was entirely devoid of adversity. When she was five years old, her parents divorced, and they were never compatible while married. After the divorce, Betty was raised by her mother, and by the time she was 8 years old, her father was absent from her life altogether.

The marriage between Betty's parents had been destined for failure from the start, and it was an arranged pairing borne out of cultural expectations. Betty's mother, Nathalie Weinstein-Bacal, was born in Romania and arrived in Ellis Island when she was between one and two years of age. She was accompanied by her parents, older brother, and younger sister, and upon arriving, her family dropped the second part of the name and was known as the Weinsteins. The family maintained a traditional Romanian family structure, with Betty's grandfather Max working and supporting the family while his wife Sophie raised the children. From the beginning, it was difficult for Max to make ends meet, but the family kept strong ties with its Jewish roots and Max borrowed money from the United Hebrew Charities in order to pay the rent for the family apartment. Initially, Max found employment in the wheat business, but this position did not last, and he was eventually relegated to the ignominious position of serving as a pushcart laborer.

Coming from an impoverished family, there was pressure for Betty's mother to work and find a husband. After coming of age, she found a job as a secretary, the job she held when she met her future husband. In contrast with Nathalie, William was not Romanian and instead came from Polish (and possibly French) origin. He was born and raised in New Jersey, and for the 20-year-old Nathalie, it is not difficult to see why William was viewed as an attractive match. His family was well-established in the United States, and William was employed in a respectable job in the medical supplies industry. At the same time, William was highly attracted to Nathalie, who was stunningly beautiful; it was from Nathalie that Betty acquired her beauty.

Ultimately, however, marital friction developed through the personality clash between the two. Nathalie was shy and dutiful, while William was volatile, jealous, and insecure. As a result, the two were constantly in conflict. Nathalie became pregnant not long after marrying William, and Betty likely would have never been born had her parents waited even a bit longer to begin having children.

Despite the apparent discord between Nathalie and William, in the years following Betty's birth, they made every effort to provide her with a supportive family environment. It was not until Betty was six years of age that they decided to divorce, a decision that led to Betty being raised by her mother from that point forward. Immediately after the divorce, William continued to visit his daughter every Sunday, but these visits ended by the time Betty was eight years old.

After the divorce, Betty and her mother adopted Bacall as their sole last name, although the second "l" would not be added to the surname until Betty was much older. Tasked with providing for her daughter, there was no question that Nathalie would be required to work, and she placed Betty in the Highland Manor school, an all-girls boarding school in Tarrytown, New York. Matriculating at Highland Manor offered benefits and limitations. On the one hand, Betty received a strong education at the boarding school, but she was also separated from her mother and living away from home at the age of 8 is a difficult shift for any child. Meanwhile, Nathalie remained in New York City, which was located roughly an hour away by train from Highland Manor, a relatively close proximity that allowed her the opportunity to visit her daughter frequently. Nathalie took Betty out for ice cream each Sunday.

Despite living away from her parents, Betty settled into a steady routine at school and remained at High Point through grade school. She was proficient in her studies and was even allowed to skip a grade (Bacall). In the end, her experience at High Point had the unfortunate consequence of separating her from her mother, but it would be misguided to suggest that her time in boarding school was unhappy. After graduating from High Point, Betty was reunited with her mother, and it was decided that she would attend high school in New York City. At this time, Nathalie and Betty moved in with Betty's grandmother and Uncle Charlie at an apartment on 84th Street and West End Avenue and she enrolled in the Julia Richman High School, located on 67th Street and 2nd Avenue.

Moving into the crowded New York City apartment brought her in closer contact with her family and offered her amenities that were unavailable in boarding school. Betty was given her own bedroom and received constant encouragement from her family. Referring to her mother, she noted that Nathalie (and her grandmother) provided their undying support: "She was not demonstrative, but I never doubted her love and her total dedication to me. We had happy times—my grandmother cooking, singing me German songs, reading constantly in French, German, Rumanian, Russian, and English…everyone in the family had humor. Everyone was educated, they all had professions…what I learned, I learned from my mother's side." (Bacall 3).

As Bacall's words suggest, her family emphasized education. Her grandmother, who was also highly religious, went to Temple and her Uncle Charlie worked as the Assistant Corporation Counsel for New York City under Mayor LaGuardia. Everyone in the family possessed strong liberal political sentiments, and Betty would retain these values throughout her life. In a 2005 interview with Larry King, she explained, "Being a liberal is the best thing on earth you can be. You are welcoming to everyone when you're a liberal. You do not have a small mind. Little picayune things. You want to welcome everyone. Liberal, little picayune thing."

After divorcing William, Nathalie never remarried, though she did have a number of boyfriends (Bacall). Instead of remarrying and having another child, Betty's mother focused her energies on raising her daughter, and as a result, Betty was closely watched. She was prohibited from engaging in any unruly activity, and during her adolescence the family relocated to an apartment on 86th Street in the hopes that it would offer a safer environment. During her teenage years, Betty enjoyed going to the movies, and she later spoke of the impact that Bette Davis, her favorite actress, had on her: "She was my fifteen-year-old idea of perfection—fine actress, dramatic bravery, doomed tragedy, sardonic wit—all an actress should be" (Bacall 1). It is perhaps surprising that Bacall viewed Davis as the actress *par excellence*, because Davis rose to fame by playing characters who were less than sympathetic, as evidenced by her performances in films such as *Jezebel* (1938) and *The Little Foxes* (1941). Young Betty Bacall was clearly not just interested in an actress who appeared glamorous but rather one who was also more independent and strong-willed.

While in high school, Bacall's interest in acting grew, and her mother eventually agreed to allow her to enroll in the American Academy of Dramatic Arts. At the time, however, this decision was not made because Betty was interested in becoming a movie star. After all, the American Academy of Dramatic Arts was located next to Broadway and across the country from Hollywood, so naturally, the Academy offered a rigorous curriculum geared toward preparing students for a life in the theater. Bacall later wrote:

> "The curriculum of the Academy was very comprehensive and geared totally to the stage. There were rules to be observed—no employment of any kind was allowed without special permission of the board. They stressed self-discovery—studying life, as that was what acting was all about. Learning technically how to speak—how to breathe. How to use one's body to project emotion. How to analyze plays and characters. It was a marvelous place to start. My year there was very serious and every course taught me something that in one way or another I have been able to apply practically…The Academy taught me to be aware of humanity in a new way—a vital part of an actor's equipment." (Bacall 22-23).

Bacall makes it clear that even though her formal training was in theater, it was nevertheless of great utility to her as an actress. In fact, during the 1940s, there was no place to take courses geared specifically toward cinematic acting, and it was at the Academy that Bacall acquired the general skills that are frequently taken for granted but still vital to succeeding as an actress, including proper breathing and elocution. Also of note in Bacall's statement is the link she draws between acting and a heightened awareness of humanity; the Academy brought her outside of herself and her loving but guarded family background, supplying her with an increased ability to perform in roles that deviated from her own personality. As she later put it, "I finally felt that I came into my own when I went on the stage." She also noted one advantage that theater had over making movies:

"When the curtain goes up, it's ours. It's ours to project what the playwright wants to stay to an audience, what to convey and to get a response from the audience immediately. Movies are great fun and wonderful when they're good. But you never get to see them till six months after they're finished. So you never get a sense of whether they're really well liked or how good they are. And you don't really know what the finished product is going to be like, because it's a director's medium…

You never see the same show twice, never. And although we -- you have to be disciplined and you have to stick to what the final cut was, you know. And I mean one is not supposed to start creating on stage and throwing all the other actors off. So, and especially in a musical because the orchestra keeps going no matter what happens. They never stop. And so it's just the most wonderful experience. It's really thrilling. And I have been very, very lucky to have been in such great shows and "Applause" of course was the great highlight for me."

While at the Academy, Bacall was deeply immersed in the theater, but this hardly meant she lost all interest in the cinema. She continued to go to the movies on a regular basis and would later name *His Girl Friday* (1942), and especially Rosalind Russell's character in the film, as a major influence (Bacall). It is not difficult to see why the film would resonate with her; Russell's character, Hilde Johnson, offered an appealing hybrid of glamour and female independence that made the film one of the more favorable portrayals of women for an era in which they were habitually cast in roles that subordinated them to men. Regardless, as long as she was living in New York, there was no way that Bacall could have predicted that she would rise to fame as a film actress rather than on the stage.

Bacall's routine at the Academy was intense, but it was still common for students to look for supplemental employment where and when it became available. As a means of helping to cover her tuition (her mother paid for the rest), Bacall found work as a model for David Crystal at his 7th Avenue boutique, a job that lasted even after she completed her theatrical training and was relatively lucrative by paying her $30 per week (Bacall). Modeling clothing was one of the most common methods through which Academy students paid for their tuition when few acting jobs were available. Modeling served as a worthy fallback option, one that was preferable to working in a restaurant and waiting tables. Through the job, models also built on their training, and Bacall's experience working for David Crystal built upon her formal training and helped her remove any self consciousness and look natural before the public eye.

Modeling provided her with necessary income, but Betty's Jewish ethnicity proved to be a deterrent in the political climate of early-1940s America. When she was hired, the clothing company was entirely unaware that Betty was Jewish, and the company learned of that fact only after Bacall herself said she was Jewish. Even though Betty had been successful in the profession, she was still relatively expendable, and the company viewed her ethnicity as grounds for dismissal. As a result, she was fired. On the one hand, leaving the modeling profession gave Bacall the chance to focus more exclusively on her acting, but she also needed a means though which to cover her bills. After graduating from the Academy, she was hired as an usher in one of the many stage theaters owned by Lee and JJ Shubert. The position paid just a fraction of what she had previously earned, and though it was affiliated with the theater, it was clearly not a job that would help her career develop. The decision to work as an usher can only be interpreted as a testament to Bacall's continued interest in working in the entertainment industry, and in a somewhat naïve state of mind, she believed that working as an usher somehow brought her closer to working as a professional theatrical or cinematic actress. She explained, "All of this [working as an usher] came from wanting to so desperately to be someone—something, to have my own identity, my own place in life. The best thing about dreams is that youth holds on to them. I was always sure mine would come true—one of them, anyway. Clearly my fantasies resulted from my identification with movies and certain stars." (Bacall 15).

Understandably, young Betty Bacall dreamed that the entertainment industry would provide fame that could not be acquired through any other profession, but her job predictably failed to open any doors for her, and she continued to struggle to find any acting opportunities. Her first potential "break" came in 1942, when she was offered the opportunity to serve as an understudy, but working as an understudy would have meant going on tour with a relatively low possibility of actually appearing before a live audience, so she turned down the offer.

Bacall's job as an usher was eventually supplemented by her return to modeling after she accepted a job modeling for Walter Thornton. This position led to Bacall being anointed as Miss Greenwich Village, a designation that was purely due to her connection with Thornton, but after that, she was subsequently hired for a Broadway show. That show then went on tour and was performed at the Playhouse Theatre in Wilmington, Delaware and in Washington, D.C.

This experience served as a major turning point in her career, and in some respects it represents the moment in which Bacall transitioned from merely being an acting student to actually becoming a professional actress. She became acquainted with the rigors of performing for days on end and living on the road, allowing her to place the skills she had learned at the Academy into practice. However, the production did not receive favorable reviews, and Bacall was relegated to once again working as a model after that show (Bacall).

During Bacall's time at the Academy, she became involved in her first romantic relationship, dating a young actor named Kirk Douglas. At this point in time, Douglas himself was still just a student, and there was little indication that he would ever reach stardom. In fact, his emotionally-charged acting style bore little similarity to the more traditional, Stravinsky-inspired acting style taught at the Academy. Born Issur Danielovitch and coming from a Russian-Jewish family, Douglas experienced much of the same ethnic prejudice as Bacall, and both would ultimately change their names. Bacall looked back on her relationship with Douglas with fondness, but she noted that she was romantically inexperienced: "I was such a child. I really had no idea how to behave with a man. I had never had a romance—certainly never had a love affair. Nice Jewish girls stayed virgins until they were married, saved themselves for the man they were going to spend the rest of their lives with, so necking in dark corners was about my speed and I was terrified to venture into the unknown beyond that." (Bacall 26).

Considering that her own mother was divorced, it is slightly surprising that Bacall would refer to her Jewish values in such stringent terms. Still, for her to remain with Douglas, she would have needed (in her eyes, at least) to have forfeited her career and commit to him for the rest of her life. Thus, while a Lauren Bacall-Kirk Douglas marriage would have unquestionably been quite glamorous, the relationship dissolved before either reached Hollywood.

Douglas and Bacall in _Young Man With A Horn_ (1950)

Chapter 4: Bogart's Breakthrough

Thankfully for Bacall's own professional career, her future husband was finally turning the corner on his career as she grew into her teens. By 1934, Bogart's life had reached its nadir; he had incurred his father's debt, was involved in a loveless marriage, and could not find consistent employment. In light of these circumstances, many understandably wonder how Bogart was able to catapult himself to fame.

One answer is that the poverty he experienced throughout the latter part of the decade effectively shed his label as a spoiled youth. Bogart had always shunned the title, but after actually experiencing poverty, he was finally able to capture the essence of a hardened everyman. Additionally, the advent of sound cinema played an integral role in transforming Bogart's identity. If vestiges of the spoiled, bourgeois young adult remained in his appearance, they were swiftly counteracted by his throaty voice, which grew increasingly coarser through his persistent smoking habits. Bogart's appearance eventually became iconic, but his voice played at least an equal role in catapulting him to fame.

It was not until 1934 that Bogart earned his breakthrough role, and it was on the stage. While Bogart acted in the Broadway play _Invitation to Murder_ at the Theatre Marque in 1934, stage producer Arthur Hopkins learned of his role. Bogart auditioned for a role in Hopkins' _The Petrified Forest_ completely hungover and looking like he had just spent all night at a bar, which he had. But the scruffy look was exactly what Hopkins was looking for, so he decided to cast Bogart to play an escaped convict in the theatrical production of _The Petrified Forest_. Hopkins mentioned just how different Bogart looked compared to the previous roles he had performed, "When I saw the actor I was somewhat taken aback, for he was the one I never much admired. He was an antiquated juvenile who spent most of his stage life in white pants swinging a tennis racquet. He seemed as far from a cold-blooded killer as one could get, but the voice (dry and tired) persisted, and the voice was Mantee's."

The play enjoyed a long run, with 197 performances at the Broadhurst Theatre in New York City, and Bogart received critical acclaim for his realistic portrayal of a madman. His role was substantially different from the film roles that would make him famous. After all, he played a man with no moral compass and was celebrated for his ability to shock audiences, leaving viewers terrified by him rather than identifying with him. Bogart was well aware that it was his breakthrough role, claiming that the role "marked my deliverance from the ranks of the sleek, sybaritic, stiff-shirted, swallow-tailed 'smoothies' to which I seemed condemned to life."

The show's enduring run also led to _The Petrified Forest_ receiving a film adaptation from Warner Brothers, but casting for the film adaptation was not as simple as transferring the actors from the stage to the screen because there were studio politics at work. Warner Brothers felt obligated to feature their premium talent; because of the play's success, the studio envisioned the film as a major box office hit and intended to deploy their most famous actors. During this period, every studio had a different niche that was aligned with a particular genre. MGM was renowned for its musicals, but Warner Brothers was associated with gangster and crime films. The studio's most notable actors were Edward G. Robinson, George Raft, James Cagney, and Paul Muni, and all of them were associated with the gangster genre. For the film version of *The Petrified Forest*, the studio had originally wanted Edward G. Robinson to play Bogart's role. Given their substantial differences in appearance and star image, it is easy to retroactively deride the studio for intending to cast Robinson, but at this time there were few actors in Hollywood with more renown, and audiences expected to watch a Warner Brothers film with at least one major gangster actor in it.

Nevertheless, Bogart was dejected after learning that he was not going to be included in the film. In an act of desperation, he contacted Leslie Howard, with whom he had starred in the play and who was also set to star in the film, and informed him of the news. Howard had been fond of Bogart in the play and contacted Jack Warner, after which Bogart was given the role.

Publicity still shot of Bogart in *The Petrified Forest*

The film version of *The Petrified Forest* (1936) proved to be an even greater career milestone for Bogart than the play had been, not because the film garnered any acclaim but because it solidified Bogart's place with the studio. He would remain with Warner Brothers for roughly the next 15 years. Beginning with a salary of $550 per week, he would keep rising through the studio's ranks until he became the highest-paid actor in Hollywood in 1946. Bogart terrified audiences in his role as Duke Mantee, the escaped convict who takes customers at a roadside diner hostage. The film is hardly remembered today, but it was a relatively significant production that starred Bette Davis in addition to the aforementioned Bogart and Leslie Howard.

Leslie Howard and Bette Davis

One of the more interesting developments that took place during the production of *The Petrified Forest* is that Jack Warner attempted to get Bogart to adopt a stage name, but he refused. Considering his ambivalence toward the name "Humphrey," it is surprising that Bogart did not adopt a new moniker, and there is no ready explanation as to why he kept the name. After all, the reasons why the studio suggested a name change were the same reasons why Bogart had always despised his first name: it was not masculine enough. It is possible that Bogart kept his name as an act of deference toward his mother, but he never spoke fondly of her and it doesn't seem likely that he would have felt any obligation toward her. Moreover, at this point in his career, Bogart held absolutely no leverage within the film industry, particularly considering the fact that he was only in the film because the leading star had forced the studio's hand. Perhaps the best explanation is that by 1936, Bogart was no longer young and it would have been too drastic a change for someone in the middle of his life.

In a sense, the rest of the decade would prove to be Bogart's most prolific period. He had not yet reached the popularity that he would later enjoy, but there was no busier period of his career. Over the course of his career, Bogart would act in over 80 films, and the vast majority of them came during the latter half of the 1930s. As a result, it is important to remember how substantially different the film industry was during the 1930s from how it is today. After an actor signed a contract with the studio, they effectively operated as indentured servants, appearing in an unlimited number of films at the discretion of the studio, who could drop them at any point in time. For this reason, from 1936-1940, Bogart averaged a film every two months, and it was not uncommon for him to appear in multiple films at once.

Bogart was typecast as a gangster villain, which ensured that he had constant work but also prevented him from becoming a star. He was a subordinate to actors like Robinson, Cagney, and Raft, who had been involved in the gangster genre for a longer period of time. Therefore, while the 1930s were the busiest phase of his career, being relegated to a narrow character type meant that he was unable to truly display his acting talents. Bogart claimed, "I can't get in a mild discussion without turning it into an argument. There must be something in my tone of voice, or this arrogant face—something that antagonizes everybody. Nobody likes me on sight. I suppose that's why I'm cast as the heavy."

Many of the films Bogart acted in from 1936-1940 are largely forgotten, but by the end of the decade he had appeared in some of the most acclaimed films in the genre. In 1938, he appeared in *Angels with Dirty Faces* alongside James Cagney, and in 1939 he held substantial roles in *The Roaring Twenties* (also with Cagney) and *Dark Victory* (with Bette Davis). In these films, there is no mistaking that Bogart was not the leading star, but he became a more recognizable face, albeit one who was forced to assimilate within the character norms of the gangster genre.

Bogart and Cagney in *The Roaring Twenties*

During the latter half of the 1930s, major changes occurred within Bogart's personal life as well. In 1937, he divorced Mary Philips, ending their perpetually tumultuous relationship. The following year, he married Mayo Methot, another stage actress whose heavy drinking was coupled with a fiery temper. Methot was yet another woman with a personality like his mother's, but Bogart's third wife had an even more erratic temper. While at times she could be quite charming, she was also prone to immense bouts of anger and was often abusive to Bogart. Over the course of their marriage, she committed a number of incidents that in most any other marriage would have been grounds for divorce, including stabbing Bogart, threatening to kill him, and setting their house on fire. Bogart could be just as abusive, and one friend quipped, "The Bogart-Methot marriage was the sequel to the Civil War". Even the press was well aware of the marital troubles, dubbing them "the battling Bogarts", and their household also became known as Sluggy Hollow. It was one of the few places Bogart and Methot could go after awhile, because places started to ban them to avoid public fighting.

Mayo Methot would drink herself to death by the age of 47.

It is difficult to determine why Bogart was drawn to such women, but some of it may have stemmed from his inherent dislike for the bourgeois nuclear family. With nontraditional wives, Bogart prevented his life from falling into the staid rhythms of the upper crust lifestyle he had always shunned. For his part, Bogart often played it off, claiming that he liked having a jealous wife and asserting, "I wouldn't give you two cents for a dame without a temper." Besides, Bogart also had a reputation for being prickly, to the extent that plenty of people in Hollywood went out of their way to avoid him, even as the media lapped up his candid statements. He explained, "All over Hollywood, they are continually advising me, 'Oh, you mustn't say that. That will get you in a lot of trouble,' when I remark that some picture or writer or director or producer is no good."

I don't get it. If he isn't any good, why can't you say so? If more people would mention it, pretty soon it might start having some effect."

It would not be until 1940 that Bogart caught his big break. That year, he was given a prominent starring role in *They Drive by Night* (1940). Directed by Raoul Walsh, the film cast Bogart and George Raft as brothers who operate their own truck-driving business. The film marked a dramatic shift away from gangster films and toward a more socially realistic style that portrayed Bogart with greater pathos than his earlier roles. One scene in particular, in which he falls asleep behind the wheel while transporting an overloaded truck filled with cargo, is especially suspenseful and conveys Bogart and Raft as everymen forced to go to extremes to make ends meet. Although the film's chief romantic grouping is between George Raft and Ida Lupino, Bogart serves as a sympathetic co-star rather than simply acting as a foil for the leading actor, and the role is substantially more significant than his earlier ones. With *They Drive By Night*, audiences finally became exposed to a more sensitive side to the actor, a dimension that would obviously emerge even further as the decade progressed.

Bogart's next film was even more significant. After starring with him in *They Drive By Night*, Ida Lupino cast him in *High Sierra* (1941), another film that deployed elements of the gangster genre while portraying its heroes in a sympathetic light. In the film, Bogart plays a man who has just been released from prison (a motif that recalls his role in *The Petrified Forest*) and is forced into reentering the mob since they engineered his release. He is then asked to take part in a major heist and acquiesces out of desperation. The heist fails, and Bogart falls in love with Ida Lupino's character, ultimately sacrificing himself to save her at the film's conclusion. The tragic hero is a trope of the gangster film, and in this regard Bogart's death would appear to make the film a classic example of the genre. However, in most gangster films the death of the criminal signals the victory of justice, whereas in *High Sierra*, Bogart's death elicits sympathy from the viewer. Consequently, *High Sierra* had a nuanced portrayal of morality, in which the viewer is forced to think outside traditional notions of good vs. evil and consider the obstacles facing a convict who is relegated to serving in the mob even after he has outgrown it and is ready to reform.

High Sierra was not a box office sensation, but it did show Hollywood that Bogart was capable of playing a leading role. Moreover, his experience acting in the film had placed Bogart in contact with John Huston, who had written the script for Lupino's film. Although he would later enjoy a famously prolific career, at the start of the 1940s Huston had not yet directed. Fortunately for him, he had the opportunity to direct *The Maltese Falcon*, a film based on a superlative pulp fiction novel by Dashiell Hammett and for which he wrote the script. Huston knew that he wanted Bogart for the starring role of Sam Spade, a world-weary detective who cannot trust anyone and is forced to solve a mystery in which nothing is as it appears.

Huston

With *The Maltese Falcon*, Bogart fully portrayed the screen persona for which he would become an icon. Although Bogart's Sam Spade is a member of law enforcement, he also defies conventional standards of behavior and morality, as evidenced by his famous quote, "I stick my neck out for nobody." In particular, his disregard for chivalry enables him to suspect that the leading female character (played by Mary Astor) is the individual responsible for the murders that take place. In his essay "The Hero", Manny Farber offers a perceptive analysis of Bogart's character and the complications associated with the star persona:

> "The hero played by Mr. Bogart, which grew out of the gangster film and
> Dashiell Hammett detective novels, looks as though he had been knocked
> around daily and had spent his week-ends drinking himself unconscious in the
> back rooms of saloons. His favorite grimace is a hateful pulling back of the lips
> from his clenched teeth, and when his lips are together he seems to be holding
> back a mouthful of blood. The people he acts badly toward and spends his
> movie life exposing as fools are mainly underworld characters, like gangsters,
> cabaret owners and dance-hall girls (and the mayor whom he puts into office
> every year). Everything he does carries conflicting quantities of hatred and love,
> as though he felt you had just stepped on his face but hadn't meant it….He is the
> soured half of the American dream, which believes that if you are good, honest

and persevering you will win the kewpie doll".

Bogart's role renewed the focus on psychological realism that was initiated in *They Drive By Night* and *High Sierra*. While the traditional law enforcement character works to maintain the façade of the American Dream, there is the sense that Bogart's character has undergone too much suffering to subscribe to such an idea. It is as though he sees the world as it is rather than how it should be. Bogart was especially proud of the film, calling it "practically a masterpiece" and adding, "I don't have many things I'm proud of...but that's one."

Trailer image from *The Maltese Falcon*

After the success of *The Maltese Falcon*, Bogart's stock had soared, and he was now nearly on top of Hollywood. Another helpful factor for him was that the United States was fighting World War II, and many of the leading actors were fighting overseas. While actors such as Kirk Douglas, Douglas Fairbanks, and Henry Fonda were gone abroad, Bogart was too old to join in the war effort, and he took full advantage of his opportunity. At the same time, Bogart provided a challenge for the Warner Brothers studio because he offered more versatility. Stars like Edward G. Robinson, James Cagney, and George Raft were all major box office attractions, but the studio basically reprised the well-worn formula of casting them as psychotic villains. Meanwhile, with Bogart the studio had a more valuable commodity, but also one who appeared too smart to believably cast as the flawed villain.

Bogart's next film, *Casablanca* (1942), would be one of the more ambitious films for Warner Brothers, as well as a major financial commitment. Hailed as an all-time classic, *Casablanca* was recognized as the number two Hollywood film of the 20th century by the American Film Institute when they comprised their list at the century's conclusion. There are many reasons for the film's continued acclaim, and chief among these was that the film perceptively captured the nation's ambivalence about going to war while at the same time recognizing that war was unavoidable.

Trailer screenshot of Bogart and Ingrid Bergman in *Casablanca*

As mentioned earlier, Warner Brothers was not only recognized for its gangster films but also for its social realist slant, and on the surface *Casablanca* would appear to clash with this framework. There is no on-location shooting, and the interiors are easily discernible as studio sets. The film does not portray the gritty scenes of working-class life that characterized *They Drive By Night* or *High Sierra* either. Bogart played the role of Rick Blaine, an American expatriate operating a nightclub in Casablanca. After coming into possession of two tickets that grant permission to leave the country, he initially intends to take his ex-lover with him (Ilsa, played by Ingrid Bergman), but instead he eventually decides to give the tickets to Ilsa and her husband Victor (played by Paul Henreid), who the police want to arrest on specious charges. By refusing to leave the country with his beloved Ilsa, the film forgoes the classical narrative trope of the protagonist and heroine uniting at the film's conclusion. Instead, Bogart's character ends the film in much the same way as in *Maltese Falcon*: alone and world-weary.

The plot borrows heavily from other genres. First, the reconciliation between Rick and Ilsa superficially resembles the comedy-of-remarriage films that involved a romantic couple reuniting. Meanwhile, the cat-and-mouse game between the virtuous Laszlo and the villainous Vichy Captain Louis Renault recalls the Warner Brothers gangster films of the preceding decade. As Manny Farber writes, "Before allied troops made it more famous, Casablanca served as a jumping-off spot to America for many of Europe's refugees—therefore a timely place to carry on Warner's favorite cops and robbers." Still, while it borrows from many different genres, the film derives its power through its ability to avoid the good vs. evil dichotomy that characterizes most gangster films. The zaniness of gangster films and screwball comedies is eschewed, and the film pours on as much emotion as possible.

One of the confounding (and appealing) aspects of *Casablanca* is that it achieves a level of psychological realism that few films have captured, yet it does so while adhering to an immense number of clichés. According to Umberto Eco, it is precisely through invoking an endless supply of clichés that *Casablanca* acquires its power: "But precisely because all the archetypes are here, precisely because *Casablanca* cites countless other films, and each actor plays a part played on other occasions, the resonance of intertextuality plays upon the spectator…When all the archetypes burst in shamelessly, we reach Homeric depths. Two clichés make us laugh. A hundred clichés move us."

The effect described by Eco has become even more pronounced in the years following the film's release. When the film is now screened, the audience is not only moved by the emotions specific to the film itself but also by the way in which archetypal scenes in the film (the famous "Play it Again, Sam" musical number, for example) have become embedded within American culture. For this reason, there is arguably no film that is more beloved in America, and the film completed the seemingly impossible task of outdoing *The Maltese Falcon* in terms of building Bogart's legend.

For *Casablanca*, Bogart was nominated for an Oscar, but he didn't win it. Bogart claimed he was fine with that, stating, "The best way to survive an Oscar is to never try to win another one. You've seen what happens to some Oscar winners. They spend the rest of their lives turning down scripts while searching for the great role to win another one. Hell, I hope I'm never even nominated again. It's meat-and-potato roles for me from now on."

Chapter 5: Bogie Meets Betty

Following *Casablanca*, Bogart finally broke his streak of successes by acting in four films of relatively minor acclaim, and his next significant film would not come until years later with *To Have and Have Not* (1944), a film that was directed by Howard Hawks and co-starred his future wife, Lauren Bacall.

It was thanks to Hawks that Bogart was even in position to meet Bacall, and one of the great ironies of Bacall's career is that it was not her theatrical work but rather her modeling that facilitated her entry into the film industry. In 1943, she had the good fortune of being placed on the cover of *Harper's Bazaar* after Diane Vreeland, the fashion director for the publication, became entranced by her extraordinarily sensual and exotic look. (Wagman-Geller). Being placed on the cover of such a major publication gave Bacall a greater forum than she had received to this point, and she caught the attention of Nancy Hawks, the wife of famous Hollywood director Howard Hawks. Nancy recommended to her husband that she arrange for Bacall to have a screen test, which eventually led to her being invited to travel to Hollywood (Wagman-Geller). After her screen test was successful, she signed a seven-year deal paying her $100 per week, substantially more than she had made even while modeling for David Crystal.

Over the last several decades, Howard Hawks has acquired a reputation placing him nearly on the same level as Alfred Hitchcock, John Ford, and other directors at the very top of the Hollywood pantheon, but when Bacall signed her contract in 1943, Hawks had not yet acquired the acclaim he would later enjoy. Still, he already held considerable clout, and it's not difficult to see why Bacall was drawn to working for him; after all, he had directed *His Girl Friday* one year prior. Still, working for Hawks meant submitting to his every whim, and the notoriously meddlesome director essentially assumed total control over her career. Bacall's role was basically that of an indentured servant, although it should be noted that this was not entirely dissimilar from the status most actors had at the height of the studio era.

Bacall with Howard Hawks in 1943

Like many famous actresses, Betty Bacall's name changed when she arrived in Hollywood. Hawks insisted that Bacall change her name from Betty to Lauren, and by this time, she and her mother had already added the second "l" to their last name. Bacall explained the dynamic she had with Hawks to Larry King in 2005, along with how the name change came about:

"KING: How did Betty become Lauren?

BACALL: I was Betty Bacall always. And Lauren was Howard Hawks.

KING: He named you?

BACALL: He named me. He liked the sound of it. And I said, well, all right. I felt a little odd about it. I don't understand all that name changing business anyway.

KING: You like Betty?

BACALL: Well, I don't like it, but it's the way it was. So you know. Stuck with the way things are.

KING: Was this for your first film?

BACALL: Yes.

KING: Howard Hawks said, change your name.

BACALL: No, he felt that Lauren Bacall was better sounding than Betty Bacall. He had a vision of his own. He was a svengali. He wanted to mold me. He wanted to control me. And he did until Mr. Bogart got involved."

Nancy Hawks was also highly involved in Lauren's career, and she would serve as a primary source of guidance (Sperber and Lax). She was particularly influential in fashion and helped Bacall present herself in a favorable light. In short, Bacall's career owed a great debt to both Howard and Nancy Hawks, the former for his clout within the industry and the latter for discovering Lauren and nurturing her upon her arrival in Hollywood.

There is no doubt that Howard Hawks saw great potential for Lauren Bacall, as he would never have signed her to such a lengthy contract otherwise, but at the same time, his motivation for hiring Bacall was at least partially motivated by his own physical attraction to her. He had every intention of romancing the 19 year-old Bacall, yet ironically enough, he would be responsible for introducing Lauren to her future husband. In 1943, Hawks and Bacall were on the set of *Passage to Marseilles*, a Warner Brothers film starring Humphrey Bogart. Hawks knew Bogart and introduced the famous actor to Bacall, and from the outset, there was a mutual attraction. Any hopes Hawks had held for romancing his young actress were effectively dashed right then and there. Lauren described the gradual nature of their relationship, "I was 19. I was introduced to him, how do you do? How do you do? Then we started to make the movie. And of course, I was hanging on Howard's every word because I was under contract to him. And that was -- I was a nervous wreck anyway. And Bogie was great. And he kidded around with me. And fortunately for me, I have a sense of humor and have always had that. That has stood me in very good stead. So we kind of played back and forth, which was just acting, just for fun. And I don't know what happened. I don't know. About three or four weeks into the movie, it began to change a little bit. And actually, he made the overtures. I did not. I would never have done that. He was, after all, was a married man. I was brought up not to have anything to do with married men." Despite an age difference of nearly 25 years, Bogart and Bacall were instantly smitten with each other, and Hawks would claim "Bogie fell in love with the character she played, so she had to keep playing it the rest of her life."

Bogart and Bacall

Humphrey Bogart and Lauren Bacall always displayed great chemistry when appearing in films together, and their subsequent marriage was strong, but there were major obstacles facing them both at the start of their relationship. Most prominently, Bogart was married to his third wife, and he and his wife, Mayo Methot, were one of the most prominent couples in Hollywood. In the relatively conservative climate of 1940s America, it did not reflect well on Bogart for him to be publicly associated with another woman, particularly one who was 25 years younger than him. Bogart and Bacall were still unmarried when their first film together, *To Have and Have Not* (1944), was released.

Like many films of the 1930s and 1940s, the film was adapted from a book by a major literary giant. Ostensibly, *To Have and Have Not* served as an adaptation of the Ernest Hemingway novel of the same name, but Hawks' treatment deviated from the novel in many important ways. In fact, the film remained true to only the first fifth of the novel, and author William Faulkner was hired to assist with the script. Rather than Hemingway's novel, a more influential text was *Casablanca* (1942), the film that had catapulted Bogart to the top of Hollywood. As with *Casablanca*, *To Have and Have Not* casts Bogart as a tired American expatriate who attempts to resist taking sides politically. Over time, he decides to support the French Resistance, with this decision paralleled by the development of his romantic relationship with "Slim," Bacall's character. Fittingly, the name Slim was inspired by a commonly used nickname for Nancy Hawks.

Bacall in *To Have and Have Not*

Any analysis of Bogart's filmography must not only examine the actor himself but also the directors with whom he worked. To this end, it is important to note that the films Bogart acted in with John Huston are vastly different from those with Howard Hawks, reflecting the extent to which Bogart cannot be considered the sole author of his films. Where Huston's films are highly stylized and filmed with violence and virtuoso camera movements, Hawks' films are lighter in tone and deploy comedy to dramatic effect. In *To Have and Have Not*, Bogart and Bacall star as lovers who meet in Martinique after the collapse of France in 1940. Bogart plays a fishing-boat captain who transports members of the French resistance. While stationed in Martinique, he meets Marie "Slim" Browning (played by Bacall), with whom he falls in love.

Unlike *Casablanca*, Bogart ends the film with the love of his life, as it is implied that he and Bacall will spend the rest of their lives together. Another difference between *To Have and Have Not* and the earlier films is that Bogart displays a lighter side of his personality, referring to

Bacall by the nickname "Slim" and engaging in courtship banter with her (most famously, when Bacall's character asks him if he knows how to whistle) that is reminiscent of the screwball comedy. In a sense, Hawks cast Bogart in the most desirable way imaginable; Bogart's role is playful enough to assume the role of a traditional leading man, but also rugged enough as a sailor and hard drinker that his masculinity is also on full display.

Moreover, despite the massive age difference between Bogart and Bacall, their witty repartee reflects a dynamic in which they treat each other as equals. In fact, Bacall is the character who more aggressively pursues the other, and her physique is more athletic and domineering as well. To this end, one of the most notable aspects of the film is the way in which Bogart is able to withhold his masculinity while also treating Bacall as his equal rather than his subordinate. Part of this was a conscious effort on Bogart's part to let Bacall steal scenes. The dynamic between the two of them was so appealing to audiences in *To Have and Have Not* that parts of their second film together, the classic *The Big Sleep*, were reshot to be racier.

The flirtatious dialogue of *To Have and Have Not* is not only characteristic of Hawks' style but also particularly apropos in light of the fact that Bogart and Bacall were also in love with one another off the film set. Despite still being married to Mayo Methot, Bogart and Bacall continued to date even after the film's production. Their courtship was not well-received by Howard Hawks, who was also in love with Bacall despite being married himself. Finally, Bogart and Methot divorced each other in 1945, something that was well overdue, and a few weeks later he married Bacall. Despite being just 45 years old, Bacall was his fourth wife. They moved into a gigantic white brick mansion in the posh neighborhood of Holmby Hills, California, and Bogart was happily married for the first time in his life.

It was incredibly fortunate that Bacall's first ever film featured her in a starring role alongside Bogart; indeed, she could scarcely have selected a more flattering vehicle for herself than to appear as the romantic lead with the premier leading man in Hollywood. Since most actors and actresses were forced to toil in the lower ranks of the studio system upon their arrival in Hollywood, the trajectory of Bacall's career was highly anomalous, because the height of her career came at the very beginning, and she was never more popular or glamorous than in the several films she appeared in with Bogart.

At the same time, Bacall was taking a chance with this as her first movie. The scenes with the two stars are charged, and some of them are widely recognized as among the sexiest in film history, especially the famous sexual innuendo Bacall uses to court Bogart: "You know you don't have to act with me, Steve. You don't have to say anything, and you don't have to do anything. Not a thing. Oh, maybe just whistle. You know how to whistle, don't you, Steve? You just put your lips together and…blow." Dialogue like this was not entirely uncommon for Hawks, whose films are filled with clever quips that serve as a kind of surrogate for sex during an age in which sexual activity was entirely forbidden by the Hays Code. Hawks' penchant for clever dialogue is just one reason why he is so famous today, but there was an element of risk inherent in appearing in such a risqué film for her first role. Bacall's performance and her romance with Bogart made her an audience favorite, yet the sexual innuendo used by her character also stamped her with a reputation for being a sexually loose woman not entirely dissimilar from the femme fatale. For the rest of her career, this would be a reputation she would struggle to distance herself from, as audiences forever preferred the youthful sensuality of the character she played in her first film.

Lauren Bacall's character in *To Have and Have Not* exudes a youthful confidence that belies the pressures inherent in the role. For one thing, despite having no film credits to her name, she was tasked with starring opposite the most famous actor in Hollywood. She later admitted to having plenty of nerves, humorously noting, "I used to tremble from nerves so badly that the only way I could hold my head steady was to lower my chin practically to my chest and look up at Bogie. That was the beginning of 'The Look.'" Furthermore, Bacall's role required her to perform "How Little We Know," a song written by Johnny Mercer and Hoagy Carmichael (who was also cast in the film.) For many years, a legend circulated that Bacall did not actually sing the song but instead lip-synched it while 16 year-old Andy Williams sang (McCarthy). It has since been revealed that Bacall did in fact sing the song herself, but Williams was indeed hired in the event that Bacall would be unable to satisfactorily sing the song herself. In any event, the anecdote is significant because the fact that an adolescent male was hired as Bacall's backup indicates just how deep Bacall's voice truly was. In fact, her voice was almost like a hybrid between that of a normal man and a normal woman, and the tenor of her voice instantly became one of Bacall's defining characteristics.

On the surface, one might expect that the relationship between Bogart and Bacall would be paternalistic, especially given the difference in age and experience between the two. In fact, the massive age gap was the primary reason that Lauren's own family disapproved of the relationship (Quirk and Schoell). But it quickly becomes apparent in the Bogart and Bacall films that the dynamic between the two stars is entirely equal. Far from being subordinate to Bogart, Bacall's characters are unafraid to take the initiative and pursue Bogart's characters. For this reason, Molly Haskell considered Bogart and Bacall one of a select few screen couples that display such a balanced gender portrayal:

> "The best of the classical couples—Bacall-Bogey in *To Have and Have Not*, Hepburn-Tracy in *Adam's Rib*—bring to the screen the kind of morally and socially 'pedagogic' relationship that Lionel Trilling find in Jane Austen's characters, the 'intelligent love' in which the two characters instruct, inform, educate, and influence each other in the continuous college of love. In the confidence of mutuality, individuals grow, expand, exchange sexual characteristics. Bacall initiates the affair, Bogey is passive…The beauty of the marriage of true minds is that it allows the man to expose the feminine side of his

nature, and the woman to act on the masculine side of hers." (26).

This description, particularly the gender reversal motif, situates the Bogart and Bacall relationship so that it is almost in the tradition of the screwball comedy. While Bogart would hardly qualify as a comedic actor, films such as *To Have and Have Not* reflect the screwball comedy's emphasis on active female roles, even though Bogart was easily old enough to be Bacall's father.

The chemistry Bogart and Bacall exuded in *To Have and Have Not* was easily matched by their romance off the set. Naturally, their relationship upset Bogart's wife, Howard Hawks, and Bacall's own family. Bogart's wife, Mayo Methot, made a desperate attempt to become sober, making it all the more difficult for Bogart to rationalize divorcing her. Eventually, however, Methot was forced to realize that her husband was no longer invested in their marriage. Meanwhile, Hawks himself posed a great threat to the affair. He still had every intention of becoming romantically involved with his newly discovered star and threatened to sell her contract to the low-budget Republic Pictures. Speaking of the experience of shooting *To Have and Have Not*, actor Walter Brennan noted that Hawks was disillusioned by the affection displayed between Bogart and Bacall: "Everyone could see something was going on with those two…but I think Howard desperately wanted to believe it was just the chemistry they had as performers, all for the good of the picture, that sort of thing. Finally it dawned on him what had already dawned on everyone else—it was so damned obvious—Bogie and Betty were falling in love. He was furious—and not as easy to work with after that." (Quirk and Schoell 14).

Brennan's comment explains one of the great attractions of watching movies: the extent to which the relationship between the characters in the films parallels their off-screen rapport. In most films, there is a layer of artifice to the film because the characters are not actually intimate off the movie set. For this reason, one reason why *To Have and Have Not* (and the subsequent films with Bogart and Bacall) is so beloved is that the chemistry onscreen was commensurate with the off-screen dynamics, thereby making the film truly lifelike.

Despite Bogart's married status and the objections of Bacall's own family and director Howard Hawks, the relationship between Bacall and Bogart progressed swiftly, and they were publicly identified as a couple even before Bogart divorced Mayo Methot. But in addition to being viewed together in public, Bacall continued to make headlines independent from her future husband. On February 10, 1945, she made an appearance at the National Press Club Canteen and famously sat on top of a piano while President Truman played a song on the same piano. The image reinforced her sultry image and ensured her status as one of the most erotic figures in Hollywood. Bacall would later note somewhat in jest that Truman played the piano "badly".

Bacall's first film was a hit, but all of the accolades and publicity were practically undone by her second film, *Confidential Agent* (1945). The film was disastrous from the start, and viewers certainly left theaters questioning Warner Brothers' belief that the film might succeed. The film cast Bacall as a socialite who aids protagonist Luis Denard (played by Charles Boyer), a concert musician pursued by fascists during the Spanish Civil War. Bacall and Boyard were a poor match, as Boyer's stodgy demeanor inevitably prevented Bacall from displaying the sensuous energy that had memorably marked her performance in *To Have and Have Not*. To her credit, Bacall knew that the film was destined for failure and attempted to remove herself from the project, but the contractual constraints inherent in being a contract player forced her to appear in it (Bacall). Predictably, the film was critically panned, and Bacall herself has claimed that her career never fully rebounded from the disastrous effects of her second movie. Whether or not this judgment is correct is impossible to determine, but the failure of *Confidential Agent* made it difficult for Bacall to prove to critics and public alike that she could succeed without Bogart at her side.

Fortunately for Bacall, by the time the movie was released, Bacall had already married Bogart, and as such, she was guaranteed of at least benefitting from her association with her famous spouse. After years of unhappily being married to Methot, Bogart had finally divorced her early in 1945, and he and Bacall married on May 21, 1945. The ceremony took place at Malabar Farm in Lucas, Ohio; the unlikely location was the home of Bogart's good friend, Pulitzer Prize-winning journalist Louis Bromfield. After the honeymoon, Bogart and Bacall settled into a large home in Holmby Hills, California, a posh neighborhood just west of Los Angeles.

Naturally, after becoming man and wife, Bogart and Bacall became inextricably linked in the public eye, and they appeared alongside one another on multiple occasions before the end of the decade. Working with Hawks proved to be a wise move, and despite their conflict over their shared love interest, the Bogart, Hawks and Bacall triumvirate reunited once again for *The Big Sleep* (1946). Adapted from a novel by Raymond Chandler, the plot borrows elements from *The Maltese Falcon*. Bogart again played a detective (Philip Marlowe), and again he is non-committal. Nevertheless, there are significant differences between the two films, extending beyond the aesthetic tendencies of the two directors. While the plot of *The Maltese Falcon* is slow and protracted, *The Big Sleep* progresses at a breakneck speed that makes it difficult for viewers to keep track of the plot developments. Bogart's Philip Marlowe saves Bacall's character, Vivian, from being prosecuted for a murder she did not commit. At the same time, Vivian is the daughter of Bogart's client, which also serves as a reminder of the age discrepancy between Bogart and his much younger wife. The film concentrates on the romance between Bogart and Bacall to the extent that the murder plot becomes almost trivial, and in this vein, Pauline Kael notes that "sophisticated sex talk became the link for the movie, and the incidents and talk were so entertaining that audiences didn't care about the solution of the murder plot." The plot is so difficult to discern that one of the central plotlines - the identity of a killer - is never actually resolved (Hare). One of the most famous anecdotes is that Hawks himself asked Chandler who killed the chauffeur, and Chandler replied, "Oh, I don't know."

Bogart and Bacall in *The Big Sleep*

As a noir, *The Big Sleep* is the more stylized film, and many consider it to be the best example of the famous pair's romantic chemistry. Foster Hirsch writes, "The quintessential Bogart-Bacall relationship occurs in *The Big Sleep*, where their feelings for each other are expressed through mutual baiting and a slicing, edgy wit...Bogart would be unable to tolerate a weepy woman...He appreciates a sarcastic dame like Bacall, who carries herself, in many ways, like one of the boys, rather than standing on ceremonies, expecting deference and courtliness where none are likely to be forthcoming." (151).

In the end, the film was another enormous success, and Humphrey Bogart was now the highest paid actor in Hollywood, commanding an unparalleled salary of $460,000. Furthermore, he commanded greater leverage in deciding on the films he appeared in. After appearing in three minor films, his next significant film was *Dark Passage* (1947), in which he plays the role of Vincent Parry, a man who has been convicted of murdering his wife and who subsequently escapes from the San Quentin Prison through a delivery truck. After meeting Irene Jansen (Bacall), Vincent falls in love with her, and they make plans to escape to South America together. It is easy to see why Bogart might have been attracted to take on the role, as there were similar plot elements to his earlier films. The escaped convict role recalls Bogart's character from *The Petrified Forest*, while the delivery truck calls to mind scenes from *They Drive By Night*. Ultimately, the film is above all a failed romance like *High Sierra*, as the romantic union between Bogart and Bacall will almost certainly be disrupted when Bogart is captured.

Building on the success of *To Have and Have Not* and *The Big Sleep*, Warner Brothers continued to pair Bogart and Bacall. However, from 1947 onward, a major shift occurred in their films, mostly because Howard Hawks was no longer hired to direct them. Instead, their next film, *Dark Passage* (1947), was directed by Delmer Daves. Of course, it would be a mistake to claim that the post-Hawks films broke away entirely from the earlier films; for example, *Dark Passage* borrowed heavily from *The Big Sleep*. Like *The Big Sleep*, *Dark Passage* was a film noire with a dark, hard-boiled plot borrowed from a pulp fiction novel. The plot was significantly easier to understand than *The Big Sleep* and featured Bacall as a painter who assists Bogart's character, a man wrongfully accused of killing his wife. However, neither the production values nor the script contained the stylistic flourishes of the earlier Bogart and Bacall films, and *Dark Passage* is best viewed as a formulaic film in the Warner Brothers film noir and gangster tradition. Since its earliest forays into sound cinema, the studio built its reputation on crime films, notably gangster films during the 1930s and noir in the 1940s. Obviously, the gangster film and film noir contain many overlaps, with one central difference being the heightened eroticism of the noir films (Gunning). It was this more explicit eroticism that served Bacall well, and she is one of a collection of famous 1940s actresses—a group that includes Rita Hayworth, Gloria Graham, Gene Tierney, and others—that are aligned with the genre.

After *Dark Passage*, Bogart returned to Huston and appeared in *The Treasure of the Sierra Madre* (1948). It had been seven years since Bogart and Huston had joined forces in *The Maltese Falcon*, and now they were both giants in Hollywood. In light of this, it may come as a surprise that *The Treasure of the Sierra Madre* does not have the polish of the earlier film, but similar to *Dark Passage*, Bogart draws from the manic energy that had characterized his earliest films. In the film, he plays Dobbs, a man who goes to the Sierra Madre Mountains in Mexico with a friend to look for gold. Although he finds an ample amount of gold, he is consumed by paranoia and later killed. The film's methodical pace raises suspense in a manner similar to *The Maltese Falcon*, but the two films are quite different. While the earlier film featured Bogart in the smartest role, the later film casts him as someone who is psychologically weak enough to let himself become overrun with irrational fear. Consequently, much of the film's success depends on whether the viewer is able to convincingly accept Bogart as capable of such mental instability. Not surprisingly, the film is more divisive than Bogart's other acclaimed works, since it was a daring departure away from the traditional Hollywood narrative structured around the formation of the romantic couple.

Publicity still from *Treasure of the Sierra Madre*

The last of the Bogart and Bacall films was *Key Largo* (1948), directed by Bogart's favorite director, John Huston. The film is relatively anomalous among the films made with Bogart and Bacall, both because it was the only one of the films directed by Huston and because the film is ideologically dissimilar from the earlier films. On its own merits, *Key Largo* is tremendously popular, largely because of its star power, which also famous stars like Edward G. Robinson, Lionel Barrymore, and Claire Trevor. The plot involves a former army Major, Frank (Bogart), who arrives in Key Largo in order to meet Nora Temple (Bacall), the wife of a deceased soldier (George Temple) he fought with in the army. While in Florida, he stays at the hotel owned by Nora's father and realizes that it has become overrun by a gangster and his mobsters. While Bogart's character looks to discover the identities of the mobsters, the town's actual law enforcement officials (a sheriff and his deputy) engage in the relatively trivial pursuit of hunting down stray Native Americans who have escaped from justice. The film centers on Frank's decision to defeat the mobster, and there is also (inevitably) a romantic plot that sees Frank and Nora together at the end.

Bacall and Edward G. Robinson in *Key Largo*)

Key Largo is very much a post-war film that addresses the horrors of killing (it is ambiguous how many men Frank has killed, but the experience has left him weary), as well as the difficulties associated with losing a spouse in the war. However, the film is also remarkably similar to *The Maltese Falcon* in its slow pacing and casting of Bogart in a role where he is outnumbered by villains whom he ultimately defeats. Additionally, the film serves as a commentary on the fall of the gangster genre, a motif that makes the film feel as though it were made a decade earlier. By defeating Johnny Rocco, who is played by an actor who had dominated Bogart early in his career, Bogart effectively usurps his early gangster roles and turns the tables on the subservient role he had played throughout the 1930s.

Bogart and Bacall in *Key Largo*

Key Largo is easily the most divisive of the Bogart and Bacall films, enjoying neither the universal acclaim of the films directed by Howard Hawks nor the general disinterest of *Dark Victory*. Some viewers hold *Key Largo* in high regard, yet more academic viewers have found much to criticize. Specifically, the film's treatment of the Native Americans living in Key Largo is patronizing at best and largely discriminatory. Furthermore, unlike the Hawks films, Bogart is very much the dominant figure. Discussing *Key Largo* in conjunction with *To Have and Have Not* and *The Big Sleep*, Molly Haskell laments the gender politics of the later film, writing, "Interestingly, Bogey and Bacall display nothing like the same excitement when they are paired again in John Huston's *Key Largo*. Here a 'more mature' Bacall is but a pale facsimile of her former self, the dazzling adult woman of her first film, *To Have and Have Not*" (20). This distinction exposes how Bogart and Bacall had superior chemistry when they were rivals than when they were on the same page.

If Lauren Bacall's role in *Key Largo* is perhaps not as interesting as the movies she appeared in earlier in the decade, the film remains one of the most studied of her films due to its pertinent allegorical themes. In this vein, it is instructive to note that *Key Largo* was made at a time in which Hollywood was becoming increasingly sensitive to the presence of Communists, with the House Un-American Activities Committee holding its infamous trials early in the following decade. More than her other films, *Key Largo* is a valuable resource insofar as it allows viewers to chart where Lauren Bacall (and Humphrey Bogart) stood on the liberal political spectrum. Director John Huston and screenwriter Richard Brooks were extreme leftists, and the film functions as an allegory for the conservative paranoia that subsumed Hollywood at the time. In particular, the relatively insignificant hunt for the Native Americans corresponds with unproductive hunt for Communists that was taking place in Hollywood:

> "The sheriff's concern with tracking down the Indians finds its parallel in the post-war witch-hunts, which seek phantom "Reds" while the really dangerous elements in society—hoodlums in both the film and real life—are free to come and go as they please and do as they like. Huston and screenwriter Brooks are suggesting that the sacrifice made by people like George Temple will have been in vain if the democratic values extolled and shared in the 1930s are replaced by those of the hoodlum, another symbol of the last decade." (Humphries 113).

Thus, *Key Largo* is regressive in terms of gender politics, but it was also a salient commentary on the contemporary political environment in America. The fact that Bogart was great friends with Huston is also extremely relevant. He had worked with Huston on *The Maltese Falcon* (1941), *Across the Pacific* (1942), and *The Treasure of the Sierra Madre* (1948) by the time *Key Largo* was released, and he and Huston shared a deep commitment to the liberal cause. By appearing in the film, Bogart and Bacall effectively declared themselves to be leftists, at a time in which Hollywood began becoming more and more conservative.

During the late 1940s, Bogart also became more politically active. He had always shunned the conservative politics of his parents, even after becoming incredibly rich himself, and the liberal ideology prevalent in Hollywood at the time cohered with his own views. Humphrey advocated on behalf of his colleagues in defense against the House Committee on Un-American Activities, which grew powerful during the Red Scare in the 1950s. At the same time, Bogart was quick to distance himself from the Hollywood Ten, a move that was instrumental in preserving his good name within the industry. He wrote an article for *Photoplay* in which he took pains to point out, "I'm no communist."

Key Largo was the last of the Bogart and Bacall films, and the subsequent years tested her ability to serve as a leading lady without her famous husband sharing the screen with her. Her career was also briefly placed on hold when she became pregnant in 1948. The child, named Stephen Humphrey Bogart, was born on January 6, 1949, and due to her parenting responsibilities, Lauren did not appear in any films during the remainder of the year. In 1950, she was cast with her first boyfriend, Kirk Douglas, in *Young Man with a Horn*. Directed by German expatriate Michael Curtiz, the film casts Lauren Bacall and Doris Day as friends and rivals who both become romantically involved with Douglas' character. In a role that shares little with her earlier ones, Bacall stars as a career-oriented woman, Amy, who studies to become a psychiatrist.

Meanwhile, Doris Day's character, Jo, is a nightclub singer. Douglas plays Rick Martin, a trumpet player, and in the end Rick and Jo are united.

Young Man with a Horn was relatively well-received but is now basically forgotten. That said, it displays a contrast between Bacall and Doris Day. While Bacall is cast as a fiery and intelligent career woman, Doris Day is the far more motherly, nurturing figure. This contrast is not entirely dissimilar from the depiction of Bacall as a femme fatale that surfaced during the previous decade; in both cases, she plays someone who is not reliant on a male presence for her happiness. It is also pertinent that Bacall plays an aspiring psychiatrist, reflecting the extreme influence of Freud on Hollywood and American popular culture during the 1940s and early 1950s.

As positive as the 1940s were for Lauren Bacall, the 1950s would be the opposite. She was still just in her late 20s, yet she now found herself unable to get any meaningful roles. Unlike other stars, Lauren was also unyielding and refused to appear in any films she deemed unworthy. Consequently, there was a sharp decrease in productivity during the early 1950s, and she did not appear in a single film from 1951-1953. During this period, a second child, Leslie Bogart, was born, and Bacall's acting hiatus gave her the opportunity to spend more time with her children.

Chapter 6: The 1950s

"When I chose to be an actor I knew I'd be working in the spotlight. I also knew that the higher a monkey climbs the more you can see of his tail. So I keep my sense of humor and go right on leading my life and enjoying it. I wouldn't trade places with anybody." – Humphrey Bogart

In addition to becoming a father, Bogart also started his own production company, called Santana Productions. Bogart's decision was met with hostility by Jack Warner; after all, the late 1940s and the 1950s were a difficult time for Hollywood studios because the emergence of television limited the box office totals and fewer major stars were willing to attach themselves to studios. For Bogart though, the idea of operating his own production company was understandably appealing. For years, he had served as a cog in the Warner Brothers machine, taking on many roles he didn't care about. Starting Santana Productions was also in line with the independent-minded characters he portrayed.

In 1949, Bogart's first films from Santana Productions were released: *Knock on Any Door* (1949) and *Tokyo Joe* (1949). They were followed in 1950 with *Chain Lightning* (1950). These were all relatively unremarkable films, but *Knock on Any Door* put Bogart into contact with Nicholas Ray, a precocious young director who blended the punchy style of John Huston with more expressive formal techniques. Huston was an "actor's director" who favored a motionless camera, while Ray was fond of experimenting with camera angles, heights, and, in his later films, color. Satisfied with the experience of *Knock on Any Door*, Bogart's would again appear in a film directed by Ray, and the film, *In a Lonely Place*, stands as one of his most renowned performances. Bogart's character, Dixon Steele, is an alcoholic writer with a tendency toward acting abusive. He is accused of committing a murder he did not commit, but his erratic behavior draws suspicion from those around him, including his girlfriend. The film juxtaposes scenes in which Steele behaves endearingly with those in which he is abusive. Even though he is eventually exonerated from the crime, his behavior ultimately ruins his relationship.

In a Lonely Place harkens back to the pre-Bacall films in that the film does not end with romantic union. Instead, the film explores the effects of a violent temper both professionally (affecting Steele's productivity as a writer) and personally (he cannot sustain a relationship.) Bogart's character resonates as someone with a utopian desire to escape the constraints of his own paranoia and the conflicts (most notably, the murder accusation that has been leveled towards him) that are imposed on him from the outside world. It sounds somewhat autobiographical too, something actress Louise Brooks picked up on in noting, "[H]e played one fascinatingly complex character...in a film whose title perfectly defined Humphrey's own isolation among people. *In a Lonely Place* gave him a role that he could play with complexity because the film character's, the screenwriter's, pride in his art, his selfishness, his drunkenness, his lack of energy, stabbed with lightning strokes of violence, were shared equally by the real Bogart."

The duality between Bogart's calm and angry temperaments in the film corresponds with Richard Schickel's belief that beneath his gruff façade, Bogart always had a romantic side that was underexplored in his films. Schickel wrote, "In many of these pictures he was woefully miscast as a 'tough guy,' rather than what he was—a romantic hiding his true nature under a gruff and sardonic shell." Certainly, the dichotomy that Schickel sees between the hardened, tough individual and the sweet romantic is on display with *In a Lonely Place*, but it is ultimately Bogart's violent side that overcomes him in the film.

Still photo from *In a Lonely Place*

After *In a Lonely Place*, Bogart teamed up with John Huston one last time, in a film that was not produced by Santana Productions but instead by United Artists, a studio that had been founded roughly three decades before by a group of actors that included Charlie Chaplin. The ambitious film, *The African Queen* (1951), was the first Technicolor film in which Bogart appeared and featured him alongside Katherine Hepburn. The plot involved sinking a German gunboat on the rivers of German-controlled East Africa during World War I. Bogart plays Canadian Charlie Allnut, while Hepburn's character is Rose Sayer, a British missionary. Over the course of the film, they become romantic while also managing to sink the German boat through a plot engineered by Rose.

More than *In a Lonely Place*, *The African Queen* conveys Bogart's romantic side. In fact, the plot line is based around Charlie shedding his tough exterior. By collectively sinking the German boat, the film displays the romantic belief that love between two people can solve any obstacle. The film builds on the romantic side of Bogart that had emerged with through *In a Lonely Place*. Hepburn and Bogart were an interesting pairing too, since she had spent much of her career appearing in screwball comedy films and he had acted in gangster films. They were thus equals and opposites at the same time, two individuals who finally united at a time in which they were beginning to grow old in front of the camera. Consequently, *The African Queen* contains an unusual balance between being an action film on the one hand (shot on location in Africa), while also a sentimental romance between two aging stars.

Hepburn and Bogart in *The African Queen*

The African Queen was a major success for Bogart, and he was awarded his first Academy Award for that performance. However, the film's production was exhaustive and took its toll on the actors. The crew lived on canned food and became ravaged by disease. Hepburn had serious difficulties with the conditions. Nevertheless, the setting on the water rekindled Bogart's love for boats, and he bought a large boat upon returning to the United States. The boat immediately became an integral part of his lifestyle, and he went on short trips nearly every day, balancing work with play in his own singular style.

After *The African Queen*, the next major film in which Bogart appeared was *The Barefoot Contessa*, directed by Joseph Mankiewicz and co-starring Ava Gardner. The film built on the autobiographical bent of *In a Lonely Place*, again casting Humphrey as an artist. He plays Harry Dawes, a film writer and director who works for an oppressive producer. Dawes directs Maria (played by Gardner), and the conflict involves Maria's discontent with being pregnant. In the end, the film is a tragedy, and Dawes is unable to prevent Maria from being killed. As with *In a Lonely Place*, Bogart is an unlikely choice to play the part of an artist. After all, it is difficult to envision Sam Spade or Philip Marlowe watching a movie, let alone writing or directing one. Even so, it is also true that even in his "tough guy" roles, Bogart has a dignified face and an articulate manner of speaking. Critic Stefan Kanfer noted that no matter how far he tried to dissociate himself from his parents, Bogart was never able to full cast aside vestiges of his bourgeois upbringing. He wrote:

> "For all his rebellions against Maud and Belmont, for all his drunken sprees and surly postures, Humphrey could not escape the central fact of his life. He was the scion of straightlaced parents whose roots were in another time. Their customs and attitudes may have become outmoded, but they were deeply

ingrained in their son no matter how hard he tried to escape them. They showed in his upright carriage and in his careful manner of speaking, in his courtesy to women and his frank dealing with men."

In many respects, Bogart was the quintessential modern hero, exhibiting a sometimes precarious balance between desirable and detrimental qualities. However, roles such as *The Barefoot Contessa* attest to the validity of Kanfer's claim. While he still assumes the world-weary feel of his earlier films, he also exudes an eloquence that recalls his privileged upbringing.

Also in 1954, Bogart appeared in the big-budget film *The Caine Mutiny*. In the film, which was Bogart's last major box-office success, he plays Lieutenant Commander Phillip Queeg, a disciplinarian who takes control over the eponymous World War II minesweeper. Queeg's harsh conduct forms the basis for the narrative's conflict, which centers on whether he is insane. Despite the obvious plot differences, Bogart's performance resembles that of *In a Lonely Place* through the instances of unrestrained (and psychotic) rage. Again, the film eschews the romantic grouping characteristic of classical Hollywood narration, as Bogart is relegated to a psychologically disturbed role that gestures to his early gangster performances for Warner Brothers. Still, it is worth noting that Bogart had eagerly sought out the role, demonstrating how he preferred performances that were psychologically unsettling and deviated from the standards for a Hollywood leading man.

Meanwhile, it was not until *How to Marry a Millionaire* that Bacall returned to the movies. The massive blockbuster production teamed Lauren up with Marilyn Monroe (who was still very young and had yet to acquire the popularity she would later receive) and Betty Grable. The three famous actresses play gold diggers who share a rented apartment, living together with the full intention of finding a wealthy suitor. Bacall's character, Schatze Page, eventually overcomes her shallow fixation toward wealth, only to eventually marry a man she does not realize is wealthy. The film is a comedy and was a major hit with audiences, but it did not flatter Lauren Bacall, because Schatze's aloof interaction with the other characters painted Bacall in a poor light. One of the pitfalls of being an actress is that audiences have a tendency to assume that the behavior of a particular character reflects their behavior off the set as well, and this dynamic had an unfortunate effect on Bacall. The youthful energy of Bacall's early films with Bogart and Hawks was replaced with a perception of her as a rather snobbish individual who had difficulty getting along with others. Even though *How to Marry a Millionaire* squarely put Lauren back on the map, it had a somewhat negative effect on her reputation.

As the 1950s progressed, Lauren Bacall abdicated her place among the highest strata of Hollywood's box office attractions, but she still managed to appear in some high-profile films and had the opportunity to work with high-profile directors, most notably Douglas Sirk and Vincente Minnelli. Bacall acted in Sirk's 1956 film *Written on the Wind*, which has been canonized as being one of the preeminent films of the decade. In an all-star ensemble cast featuring Robert Stack, Rock Hudson, and Dorothy Malone, Bacall plays secretary Lucy Moore. The narrative centers on a tangled web of romances that eventually sees Bacall's character united with Rock Hudson. *Written on the Wind* is most memorable for Sirk's highly eccentric formal technique; the director was famously known for making expressive use of distancing techniques such as filming with mirrors in the background and using highly saturated colors. The almost campy production values heighten the melodramatic plot, making the film one of the more notable tearjerkers of the decade. In an almost hyperbolically emotional plot, Bacall's character is surprisingly subdued, and she no longer showcases the energy of her earlier roles. The film thus provided further proof that by the mid-1950s, Bacall had shifted from youthful roles to ones that featured her as an elegant yet somewhat conservative figure.

Bacall in *Written on the Wind*

Bacall followed *Written on the Wind* with *Designing Woman* (1957), which paired her with Gregory Peck. Her character, Marilla Brown Hagen, is a fashion designer who marries sportswriter Mike Hagen (Peck) despite having known him only for a short while. The role was a clear departure from Bacall's femme fatale performances from the previous decade, and in this regard it continued the tendency toward casting her in a more socially "proper" role. At the same time, the film clearly capitalizes on Bacall's statuesque physique, and it is difficult to argue against the notion that Lauren was ideally suited for the role of a fashion designer. It was also quite progressive for Bacall to play a career woman in the context of 1950s Hollywood. Even so, Bacall and Peck never appear entirely comfortable together, prompting viewers to yearn for the more exciting Bogart and Bacall films of the previous decade. The sparring that occurs between the two characters is almost akin to the screwball comedy, but the film is not humorous enough (or biting enough) to assimilate within the genre.

The film is also notable for having been directed by Vincente Minnelli, who was famous for *Gone With The Wind* and had also directed Bacall in *The Cobweb* (1955). Like Sirk, Minnelli was famous for his sumptuous cinematography, replete with lavish set designs. Accordingly, *Designing Woman* is at the very least enjoyable on a visual level, although Emmanuel Levy correctly notes that the visuals (and attempt at screwball comedy) do not compensate for the uninspired script: "Aiming to recapture the sleekness of Hollywood's 1930s and 1940s screwball comedies, the film had the glossy look of studio-manufactured entertainment. *Designing Woman* emphasized high production values at the expense of an original screenplay" (291). Despite its limitations, the film stands as one of the more important of the decade for Bacall, not only because of the opportunity to work with Gregory Peck and Vincente Minnelli but because she plays a headstrong career woman.

Unfortunately, as the 1950s progressed, Bogart's health began to quickly deteriorate. Despite only being in his mid-50s, he was diagnosed with esophageal cancer, likely the result of his heavy smoking and drinking. The shift in his health was swift and immediate; in the years prior, he and Bacall had been one of the more high-profile couples in Hollywood. In fact, Bogart and Bacall were founding members of the Rat Pack in Las Vegas, a development that arose through Bogart's love for drinking and the couple's friendship with Frank Sinatra. After being diagnosed with cancer, Bogart went from public displays of drinking and easy living with his Rat Pack mates to falling deathly ill at the hands of his favorite vices. The Rat Pack would rise to fame after Bogart's death, highlighted by the film *Ocean's Eleven* (1960), and all the while they maintained a legacy of hard drinking and easy living.

Dean Martin and Frank Sinatra were both part of the Rat Pack

Bogart's last film was *The Harder They Fall* (1956), directed by Mark Robson. A notable director in his own right, Robson specialized in social realist films during the 1940s, and his style would have been an ideal match for a younger Bogart. In *The Harder They Fall*, Humphrey plays Eddie Willis, an impoverished sportswriter who becomes involved in fixing boxing matches and eventually becomes ashamed and publicizes the seedy injustices of the sports gambling industry.

The Harder They Fall was particularly difficult for Bogart, as he had become quite ill by the time the film was made. In March 1956, he had his esophagus, two lymph nodes, and a rib removed. Unable to make any more films, his life and career ended in concert. Instead of making any additional films during that year, 1956 was spent saying farewells to his family and acquaintances. He took his poor health in stride, and even had his dumbwaiter custom designed so that he could ride in a wheelchair up and down to get around: "Put me in the dumbwaiter and I'll ride down to the first floor in style."

Bogart lasted for one year after his diagnosis, finally passing away on January 14, 1957. By then, his 57 year old body had withered to just 80 pounds. Huston gave the eulogy at Bogart's family and said:

> "Bogie's hospitality went far beyond food and drink. He fed a guest's spirit as was well as his body, plied him with good will until he became drunk in the heart as well as his legs…Himself, he never took too seriously—his work most seriously. He regarded the somewhat gaudy figure of Bogart, the star, with an amused cynicism; Bogart, the actor, he held in deep respect...In each of the fountains at Versailles there is a pike which keeps all the carp active; otherwise they would grow overfat and die. Bogie took rare delight in performing a similar duty in the fountains of Hollywood. Yet his victims seldom bore him any malice, and when they did, not for long. His shafts were fashioned only to stick into the outer layer of complacency, and not to penetrate through to the regions of the spirit where real injuries are done...He is quite irreplaceable. There will never be another like him."

After Bogart's death, Bacall found herself a widow at the young age of 34. She explained, "[L]osing Bogey was horrible, obviously. Because he was young. And because he gave me my life…I don't know what would have happened to me if I hadn't met him. I would have had a completely different kind of life. He changed me, he gave me everything. And he was an extraordinary man."

Despite mourning heavily over the premature death of her husband, she began dating shortly thereafter, and she was romantically linked to Frank Sinatra in the immediate aftermath of the tragedy. It is not difficult to understand how she and Sinatra became lovers, especially given that they were good friends for years. Like with Bogart, the relationship between Bacall and Sinatra progressed swiftly, and they even considered marriage. Ultimately, however, their relationship disintegrated as quickly as it began. The exact cause for the conflict is ambiguous, but Bacall insisted that the separation was due to her own frustration with Sinatra's notorious womanizing. As she put it, Sinatra was a "womanizer" who "wanted to be in the sack with everybody."

From 1957 onward, Bacall's acting output became increasingly sporadic. She continued to experience difficulty finding attractive film acting opportunities, so she turned to the theater. While that sounds like a step down, Bacall's original training had been in theater, so she was not disappointed by the change. She did not disavow cinema entirely, but as she entered her middle age years, the ratio between her film and theater performances became more even. In 1959, she starred in the Broadway production of *Goodbye, Charlie*, and 1965 saw her appear in the Broadway play *Cactus Flower* (1965). Meanwhile, her 1960s film roles were mostly minor performances in big-budget Hollywood movies. In 1964, she appeared in *Sex and the Single Girl*, a romantic comedy in which she played the wife of Henry Fonda. The film was one of the most commercially successful films of 1964, but its popularity should not be interpreted as a sign that Lauren Bacall had reentered the highest ranks of Hollywood. Not only was she not cast as the romantic lead (an honor that went to Natalie Wood), but she plays a character who is decidedly middle age, a designation that essentially excluded her from serving as the film's primary box office attraction. In 1966, Bacall appeared in another big-budget film when she acted in *Harper*, playing a wife whose husband has gone missing. As with *Sex and the Single Girl*, Bacall does not occupy the leading role but instead demonstrated her ability to serve a supporting role amidst a large ensemble cast.

For the most part, Bacall's career remained relatively nondescript during the 1960s, but her personal life underwent significant changes. It is often forgotten that Humphrey Bogart was not the only celebrity husband of Lauren Bacall's, because she was married to actor Jason Robards during the 1960s. This marriage, which began in 1961, was more tumultuous than her time with Bogart, mainly due to Robards' alcoholism, but the marriage lasted nearly as long as her first one, and she also gave birth to her third child, Sam Robards. Much of Bacall's waning productivity as an actress during the decade can be attributed to the fact that she was in the process of raising three children. Bacall noted, "I put my career in second place throughout both my marriages and it suffered. I don't regret it. You make choices. If you want a good marriage, you must pay attention to that. If you want to be independent, go ahead. You can't have it all."

Eventually, Bacall and Robards divorced in 1969, but she still had fond things to say about Robards afterwards. When asked about him in the 2005 interview with Larry King, she noted, "Jason, great actor, truly great actor. And we had a marvelous time together. We did the best we could. You know. He had a slight problem. And we couldn't rise above it, unfortunately." Talking about his alcoholism, she asserted, "I don't even know if he enjoyed it, but he was hooked on it. And it really almost destroyed him. And fortunately did not."

Robards

Chapter 7: Bacall's Independent Career

"I'm not a sedentary person. I've always been active." – Lauren Bacall

The life and career of Lauren Bacall has easily identifiable stages, from her modeling career in New York City to her marriage with Bogart and her marriage to Robards. Of course, the ensuing decades have been marked by her life as a single woman. After divorcing Robards, Bacall continued to date but never again remarried. As she put it, "I don't sit around thinking that I'd like to have another husband; only another man [who] would make me think that way... Find me a man who's interesting enough to have dinner with and I'll be happy."

By 1970, Bacall was clearly aging, and she was quite different than the sultry figure who had captivated Bogart and the rest of the nation with her performance in *To Have and Have Not*. Not only was she no longer married to Bogart, but her affiliation with cinema began to loosen considerably. From 1966-1973, she did not appear in any movies, instead focusing on theater, and in 1970, she received a Tony Award for her performance in *Applause*, a play that was also notable for the fact that she and co-star Len Cariou were romantically involved. Her theatrical performances continued to receive praise, and she was honored with a second Tony Award for her role in *Woman of the Year* (1981).

Bacall's film appearances during her late career did not garner as much attention as her stage roles. As with her 1960s films, she was part of large ensemble casts that never brought her to the fore. In 1974, she played Mrs. Harriet Belinda Hubbard in an adaptation of Agatha Christie's *Murder on the Orient Express*, which also included Albert Finney, Michael York, Vanessa Redgrave, and Ingrid Bergman. Two years later, she was cast alongside John Wayne in *The Shootist* (1976), which earned her a nomination for the BAFTA Award for Best Actress and also resulted in an unlikely friendship with John Wayne. Even though Wayne was famous for his right-wing politics and Bacall has long been known for her left-wing leanings, the two had great chemistry on screen and were friendly off it.

Bacall in *Murder on the Orient Express*

Even as she entered old age, Lauren Bacall remained extremely active, and she has averaged roughly a film per year since 1980, despite the fact she took an extended hiatus and didn't appear in any films from 1981-1988. Her films during the last few decades included not only big-budget films, such as *Misery* (1990), but also art house movies such as Robert Altman's *Pret-a-Porter* (1994). In 1997, she was honored with the Kennedy Center Honors and was also nominated for (but did not win) an Academy Award for Best Supporting Actress for her role in *The Mirror Has Two Faces* (1996). This surge in popularity ensured she could continue her film career into the 21st century, during which she has acted in 13 more films.

Even as she approaches 90, Lauren Bacall's acting career is not over. She fractured her hip during the winter of 2010-11, but she still remains active and lives in her apartment on the Upper West Side of Manhattan . In 2009, she was given an Honorary Academy Award, an honor that compensated for the Academy Award that she was denied in 1997. Thus, even as she continues to be recognized for her acting accomplishments, she continues to expand her impressive oeuvre and her career is still a work-in-progress.

Chapter 8: The Legacy of Bogie and Betty

Bogart died a premature death, just three years after being nominated for an Academy Award in *The Caine Mutiny*, but it is worth considering whether his career would have remained successful. By the mid-1950s, Bogart's tough, unsentimental acting style was becoming outdated by a more sensitive acting style, a development attributable to the popularity of the Actors Studio headed by Lee Strasberg in New York City. While Bogart displayed little emotion, actors like Marlon Brando and James Dean won audiences over with sweeping portrayals of sensitive, disturbed characters. Had Bogart's career continued, he almost certainly would have continued to find consistent employment, but it is likely that his days as a leading man were coming to an end, regardless of his cancer.

Bogart's legacy has only grown in size since his death, and today it extends well beyond his iconic character type and roles in films like *The Maltese Falcon*, *Casablanca*, and *Key Largo*. While those movies inextricably linked with the crime genre as a whole, Bogart's subsequent characters (from the 1940s onward) behaved with honor but also an understanding that traditional views of morality were inadequate in the context of modern life. This helped solidify Bogart as an iconic modern hero who not only behaves virtuously but does so in an approachable, psychologically realistic manner that understands the difficulties of life. In his pseudo-obituary on Bogart, Andre Bazin describes Bogart thusly: "Humphrey Bogart was a modern hero. The period film—the historical romance or pirate story—didn't suit him. He was the starter at the race, the man who had a revolver with only one bullet, the guy in the felt hat that he could flick a finger with to express anger or gaiety." This description in particular, treating anger and joy as twin emotions, reflects the monumental effect that he had on audiences.

In a similar vein, Bogart and his roles continue to be relevant today because of the individualistic nature that his characters had. As actor Rod Steiger put it, "Bogart has endured because in our society the family unit has gone to pieces. And here you had a guy about whom there was no doubt. There is no doubt that he is the leader. There is no doubt that he is the strong one. There is no doubt with this man that he can handle himself, that he can protect the family. This is all unconscious, but with Bogart you are secure, you never doubt that he will take care of things." This also extended to the man himself, as friend and biographer Nathaniel Benchley wrote of him, "He achieved class through his integrity and his devotion to what he thought was right. He believed in being direct, simple, and honest, all on his own terms, and this ruffled some people and endeared him to others."

Lauren Bacall's legacy is predominantly tied to her famous marriage with Humphrey Bogart, and the significance of the Bogie-Bacall pairing cannot be denied. Films such as *To Have and Have Not* and *The Big Sleep* were not only highly entertaining but also offered depictions of marriage that were progressive in their gender portrayals. Even though Bacall was young enough to be Bogart's daughter, she enjoys every bit as much agency as Bogart (with the exception of *Key Largo*), and an infectious chemistry—not unlike that of the screwball comedy couple—appears throughout their films. However, after Bogart's death, Bacall was unable to find another suitable romantic co-star, and Saul Asterlitz is not incorrect when he notes, "In truth, Bacall never regained the comic verve of her all-too brief collaboration with Bogart and Hawks" (387). In the end, the films Lauren Bacall appeared in with her husband are treasured not only because the films were so memorable in their own right but as a result of the fleeting nature of their famous marriage.

While there is no denying that Bacall is most remembered for her marriage to Bogart, it would be a mistake to disregard her life and career after Bogart's death, which happens all too often. After all, by focusing on her early films with her late husband, people concentrate only on the first third of her life. It is also important to account for Bacall's later years since they underline the extent to which she became a highly independent figure. It is not by accident that her first autobiography, published in 1978, was titled *Lauren Bacall By Myself* (1978). Lauren Bacall must be acknowledged not only for her most famous films but also for her open willingness to resist marriage later in life, maintaining her career instead of submitting to a traditional life of domesticity. Analyzed in its entirety, the life and career of Lauren Bacall reveal an individual who should not only be commemorated for her famous marriage and films but also for being an independent woman in her own right.

Bibliography

Austerlitz, Saul. Another Fine Mess: A History of American Film Comedy. Chicago: Chicago Review Press, 2010. Print.

Bacall, Lauren. By Myself and Then Some. New York: Caprigo, 2005. Print.

Bazin, Andre. "A Portrait of Humphrey Bogart." *The Films of My Life*. Cambridge: Da Capo Press, 1994.

Brooks, Louise. "Humphrey & Bogey." *Sight and Sound* 36.1 (Winter 1967). Accessed from http://www.psykickgirl.com/lulu/bogey.html.

Dyer, Richard. *Stars*. London: BFI, 1986.

Eco, Umberto. "Casablanca, or, The Cliches are Having a Ball," *Signs of Life in the U.S.A.: Readings on Popular Culture for Writers*, Eds. Sonia Maasik and Jack Solomon, Boston: Bedford Books, 1994, 260-264.

Farber, Manny. *Farber on Film: The Complete Film Writings of Manny Farber*. Ed. Robert Polito. New York: Library of America, 2009.

Gledhill, Christina. "Signs of Melodrama." *Stardom: Industry of Desire*. Ed. Christine Gledhill. New York: Routledge Press, 1991.

Gunning, Tom. The Films of Fritz Lang: Allegories of Vision and Modernity. London: British Film Institute, 2008. Print.

Hare, William. L.A. Noir: Nine Dark Visions of the City of Angels. Jefferson: McFarland, 2008. Print.

Haskell, Molly. From Reverence to Rape: The Treatment of Women in the Movies. Chicago: University of Chicago Press, 1987. Print.

Hirsch, Foster. The Dark Side of the Screen: Film Noir. Cambridge: Da Capo Press, 1981. Print.

Humphries, Reynold. "Ethical Commitment and Political Dissidence." John Huston: Essays on a Restless Director. Eds. Tony Tracy, Roddy Flynn. Jefferson: McFarland, 2010. Print.

Kael, Pauline. "About Comic-Strip Style, from a Sense of Disproportion." *For Keeps: 30 Years at the Movies*. 103-105.

Kanfer, Stefan. *Tough Without a Gun: The Extraordinary Life and Afterlife of Humphrey Bogart*. New York: Random House, 2011.

Levy, Emanuel. Vincente Minnelli: Hollywood's Dark Dreamer. New York: St. Martin's Press, 2009. Print.

McArthur, Colin. *Underworld, USA*. London: Secker & Warburg, 1972.

McCarthy, Todd. Howard Hawks: The Grey Fox of Hollywood. New York: Grove Press, 1997. Print.

Meyers, Jeffrey. *Bogart: A Life in Hollywood*. London: Deutsch, 1997.

Porter, Darwin. *The Secret Life of Humphrey Bogart: The Early Years (1899-1931)*. New

York: Blood Moon Productions, 2003.

Quirk, Lawrence J., and William Schoell. The Rat Pack: Neon Nights and the Kings of Cool. New York: HarperCollins, 2003. Print.

Schickel, Richard. *Bogie: A Celebration of the Life and Films of Humphrey Bogart*. London: Aurum Press Ltd., 2006.

Sperber, Ann, and Eric Lax. Bogart. New York: HarperCollins, 1997. Print.

Thomson, David. Humphrey Bogart. New York: Faber and Faber, 2009. Print.

Wagman-Geller, Marlene. And the Rest is History: The Famous (and Infamous) First Meetings of the World's Most Passionate Couples. New York: Penguin, 2011. E-Book.

15181271R00040

Made in the USA
Middletown, DE
26 October 2014